smörgåsBOARD

A cultural and edible journey into skateboarding

Josh Sutton

First published in 2023 by Red Fez Books

ISBN: 978-1-838421-2-8

Design and layout by Josh Sutton
Front Cover photo by Brendan Harrop
Illustrations & photographs, unless otherwise stated, Copyright Josh Sutton

OTHER BOOKS BY JOSH SUTTON

Guyrope Gourmet 2013
Food Worth Fighting For 2016
Outdoor Ovens 2017
Five Go Feasting 2018
CookPal 2018
Food From Childhood 2019

www.joshsutton.co.uk

CONTENTS:

INTRODUCTION

"I'M JUST DIGGING THIS TIME. THERE SHOULD BE ANOTHER TERM BESIDES "MIDLIFE CRISIS," EVERYONE LIKES TO SAY SHE/HE IS HAVING A MIDLIFE CRISIS. I'D LOVE TO REBRAND SOME VERSION OF THAT WHERE YOU START HAVING A MIDLIFE DISCOVERY OR BREAKTHROUGH."

AMY POEHLER

American psychologist, Erik Erikson was awake to the notion of discovery and breakthrough. His theory that each stage in life is associated with a particular psychological struggle, with each contributing to one's personality, opens-up such possibilities. He put forward that what he identified as 'the seventh stage' of psychological development which takes place between the ages of forty and sixty-five years, ushers-in the dichotomy of 'Generativity vs. Stagnation'. Generativity might manifest in a number, or a combination of forms; procreation, productivity and creativity. It's the productivity and creativity that I recently discovered through taking-up skateboarding for the first time, in my fifties. I think that is what Amy Poehler is referring to when she talked about a midlife discovery or breakthrough. Skateboarding for me has been, and continues to be a mid-life discovery.

I'm a food and recipe writer and part of food writing is about making new discoveries, working with new ingredients, foreign ideas and methods that from time to time lift you from your comfort zone that can take you to new places.

A recipe is a wonderful thing, it's a means of conveying information that will enable a person to mimic, or approximate, the actions of another. If the recipe is described well, then the result will be rewarding for all involved. The student can become the master as the recipe is reproduced and shared with others. A recipe doesn't necessarily have to be in written form, it may be described by demonstration. It needn't always involve food. The Romans developed a recipe for concrete over two thousand years ago. It is one that was described so well that as a result, the remains of many roman buildings are still standing to this day.

A recipe for a meal or a particular dish also has a number of other properties. When passed on and repeated, it can help preserve traditions, customs and cultures. A recipe can evoke memories, a recall of time and place of its learning. But above all, when shared, a recipe has the power to bring people together. It wasn't long before I realised the tangible connection between two of my favourite things, food and recipe writing and skateboarding. The know-how of skateboarding is shared among those who do it, described by demonstration, and honed by repetition. The knowledge is passed on from person to person, just as many old family recipes are passed on from parent to child. Couple this idea with an age old recipe for concrete, and people will gather from miles around. Therein lies the makings of a community.

People have enjoyed eating, and in particular sitting down and eating together as a family or community, ever since our hirsute ancestors ventured from their caves and first learned to forage, hunt and cook.

Skateboarding, on the other hand, is a relatively new activity, and as I have discovered, it also breeds notions of family and community among many of those who do it. Originating in the United States during the 1950s, skateboarding's popularity has waxed and waned over the intervening years. The stories of Californian surfers taking to the skateboard when the surf was flat may or may not be true, but the invention of the urethane wheel in the early 1970s led to a renaissance, paving the way for skateboarding to become a global phenomenon, to such an extent that in 2020 it debuted as an Olympic sport.

Skateboarding is now a multi-billion dollar global industry, with several equipment manufacturers, associated clothing brands and a growing number of professional skateboarders, riding a lucrative gravy train rattling, full-speed along the tracks, all the way to the bank. (please stand clear of the closing doors).

I'm relatively new to skateboarding, and at the age of fifty seven I am never likely to join the ranks of the professionals. I took up skateboarding as a fifty one year old, having grown tired of watching my (then) ten year old son ripping through our local park, having more fun than his grandmother used to at the bingo. I noticed how other, more experienced, skaters offered help and encouragement to my son, sharing their knowledge as he gradually learned new tricks and moves. Admittedly, as a parent, I was initially wary of young adults approaching him, but very quickly learned that they were just keen to pass on tips and advice, rather than hard drugs and lessons in anti-social behaviour.

After a couple of months of watching his progress, and astounded at the rate at which he was learning and becoming confident on his board, I thought i'd have a go myself. It took me a good six months to find my centre of balance, and with each visit to the park came a little more confidence. I initially bought a cruiser board, with soft wheels that make riding over rough ground a little easier, and spent the first year pushing around on the flat ground, too timid to roll down a ramp at this stage. What surprised me, almost from day one, was that the younger skaters at the park, which of course meant *every* skater at the park, were encouraging me, offering praise for my gradual progress. It was the first of many revelations to come.

Now six, almost seven, years in to my 'career', I am happy 'dropping-in' to a bowl and carving to my heart's content (or at least until my aged knees tell me to give it a rest). I got to this stage with the help of other skateboarders, people who took time to share their knowledge and experience in a non-judgemental way, offering advice on how and where to stand on the board, how to shift and adjust my weight as I approach the bottom of the ramp and quite literally holding my hand as I finally learned to 'drop in'. No-one in a skatepark has ever suggested that I might be a little old for this kind of thing.

Skateboarding has opened up a whole new world for me, a world which continues to fascinate on a daily basis. Not least as, like many counter-cultural activities, skateboarding brings with it its own lexicon. Just as beginners learn tricks, they also learn the language. It's a language that shares a degree of parity with surfing and snowboarding. It's also a language that, by virtue of the fact that many skaters are themselves young people, is associated particularly with young people. Having started skateboarding in my fifties, it took me a while to feel comfortable using terms like 'sick', 'rad' and 'dope', but now they flow naturally. A familiarity with the language seems to enhance the experience, closing the gap between newcomer and veteran. It's also a little like learning the basics, like please and thank you, in a foreign language when you go on holiday abroad. You might get charged extra for having a terrible accent, but at least you made the effort.

Whilst the doors of the gravy train may be closed to the majority, skateboarding serves as a portal to riches not measured within the narrow constraints of mere monetary value. Certainly in my own experience, as I ventured further into the world of skateboarding, the discovery of a creative and largely inclusive community, both at a local level, as well as on a global scale, has fed and fuelled my own artistic and culinary endeavours. It has reinvigorated my lust for life, leading to new friendships and experiences that I would otherwise have missed out on.

It is this experience that I wish to share, not as a boast, but as an insight into what can happen and what happened to me at a time in life when some folks are perhaps looking to slow down a little. For me learning to skateboard continues to be a challenge, not just in the physical sense as my body ages and every muscle, tendon and bone seems to ache after a good session, but also in the sense of my own mental well-being.

Mental health is a state of mental well-being that enables people to cope with the stress of life, realize their abilities, learn well and work well, and contribute to their community. It is an integral component of health and well-being that underpins our individual and collective abilities to make decisions, build relationships and shape the world we live in. - WHO 2023.

By stepping on to a skateboard at my age I made myself vulnerable, not just to injury, but to potential ridicule from younger skaters in the park as well as my peers. When that ridicule failed to materialise in the park, but rather materialised as encouragement apparent respect instead, I felt good. It made me happy. Similarly among my close adult friends, many if not most of them offered a sort of 'good on ya' response, often qualified with a chuckle and an additional, 'you mad bastard!'. Even my father, then in his late seventies and having only just given up playing squash himself, offered some of his well-rationed praise. It was without doubt a very positive response.

On the other hand, and occasionally among a broader set of acquaintances, particularly among some strangers, came what I perceived as disdain, anger and the ridicule that I had anticipated would come from people much younger than me. I put it down to jealousy and to be honest I really don't care what other people, particularly those I don't know, think of me. Skateboarding feeds me, it nurtures my mental health, and in order to carry on doing that I in turn need to feed my body. Our diet informs and affects, not just our physical capacity to perform, but also our mental capacity.

smörgåsBOARD describes a journey, a cultural and edible journey, into the world of skateboarding.

"Learning to drop-in after about a year totally blew my mind, it was like someone had just handed me a beer glass that fills itself up once you drain the last dregs from the bottom".

OLD DOG NEW TRICKS

I am an old dog, and in learning to skate you could say that I have learned a new trick, but I have to come clean here. When it comes to skateboarding, my bag of tricks is actually quite limited. I can't ollie (the trick where you slam the tail down and slide the outside edge of your front foot along the board enabling the rider to jump up steps and onto obstacles), I ride transition, the smooth curves, ramps and bowls in a skatepark. The kick flip, the one that everyone asks if a skater can do, is way beyond both my ken and capability. I have no interest in learning theses tricks, and this is purely from a self-preservation point of view. Both the ollie and the kick flip require the rider and the board to leave the ground. As far as I can see, this greatly increases the likelihood of injury, should any attempt go wrong, and injury is a thing I do my best to avoid.

"Grow up!" That's what the miserable old geezer yelled at me from his car window, turning the steering wheel slowly in his string-backed leather driving gloves. His fine trilby hat was pulled down over his eyes, restricting his field of view, but in reality I think it was his 1950s mentality obscuring his vision, rather than any dapper looking hat. I was pushing along the road, on my way to the supermarket for essential supplies during lock-down. The 56mm Ricta Clouds beneath my board were sending gentle vibrations up through my whole body, reminding me that I was still alive, and even a mundane essential trip to the supermarket and back can be a wind in the hair thrill, not that there's much of that left these days.

The pensioner, in his polished and cherished car, accelerated gently towards his dotage and out of my mind, that is until a little further down the road when I caught the mutterings of an old woman barking into her husbands ear as they shuffled from the Post Office, pension books in hand, "look at that idiot, thinks he's a kid." It seemed that I'd managed to offend some folks, old folks, folks even older than me.

What's so offensive about a guy in his fifties rolling along on a skateboard? Was it me or the board? I think the truth is that skateboards, or perhaps the perceived image of those who ride them, scare some folks; in the same way they scare small dogs that come running after you yapping and snarling at your wheels. This chorus of disapproval rang out loud, seemingly accentuated by the almost peaceful silence that came with lock-down. It was a time when keeping a safe distance also appeared to amplify our differences. Cyclists, joggers and dog walkers attract scorn from those who neither do, nor will have, any of it. But two years later, in a society now less vulnerable to the threat of that particular virulent virus, those prejudices will abate. Not so with skateboarding though, and even less so with (for want of a better phrase) senior skaters.

The day I first started skating six years ago, I inadvertently joined a unique group of adults, that is adults who learned to skate later in life, as opposed to skaters who grew up to be adults. Although skateboarding is largely perceived by many as solely an activity for the youth, thanks to social media, I soon discovered that there were others like me, older skaters who had taken it up in adulthood.

For me, learning to drop-in after about a year was a total revelation. It brought a sense of achievement that outmeasured many in my life, almost on a par with learning to drive and the freedom that brought to a seventeen year old lad living in the Yorkshire Dales. The sensation of placing the tail of your board at the top of a transition, positioning your leading foot over the front truck and leaning forward, submitting to the laws of gravity is one that is difficult to describe. I liken it to someone handing me a beer glass that fills itself up once you drain the last dregs from the bottom. From that point on I realised that I could do this again and again and I was hooked on skating. My learning to skate is not about recapturing lost youth it has little to do with age in that respect, it has more to do with curiosity, a desire for challenge, and I must admit a touch of the absurd, I've always been a bit of a show off. Skating makes me happy, it's a source of enjoyment, a challenge, a way of meeting new people and learning new things, and in many ways a meditation. It heals me.

I was curious to learn about others' experiences, what do other 'later skaters' get from it? I sought out others via social media, instagram predominantly, and began to make connections.

I asked Esther Sayers, a senior lecturer in education at Goldsmiths, University of London, whose academic interests are around arts participation, what motivates people to engage with art. She is currently exploring the various immersive pedagogies that operate within the context of the skatepark, with a particular focus on older women as a means to explore the navigation of risky behaviours, age and motherhood. Esther started skating in her late 40s.

ES: *I think it is important to make visible the area of skateboarding not as a child or as an adult that has done it for years but as older newcomers. It's not Thrasher and it's not Middle Aged Shred. We are talking about something different, something more radical I think.*

Radical maybe, but why? It strikes me that if I were to tell people that I had just returned from a skiing holiday, they would not bat an eyelid. But when I explain that our last family holiday was spent touring the skateparks of the Basque Country, people seem to think that I'm insane.

ES: *Yes!!! Our family holidays are always skate tours now but I found during the last one in Dorset that it was often me skating alone. I often out skate my kids these days – my drive is more urgent somehow. They have years left to skate, I on the other hand find every moment precious and treat it as such. It's normal to do that kind of holiday in a ski context, but not skate.*

Maybe it's to do with the fact that people seem to become more risk averse as they age, too comfortable perhaps. Me skateboarding, for example, has pissed off some of my closest people, like it's an affront somehow, messing with the status quo of age and expectations. My life outside skateboarding was already established, even too established – adulthood is constricting. Skating has helped me deconstruct the confinement of adulthood.

Adulthood can be constricting, not least because our aging bodies interfere with our capacity to perform the feats we took for granted in our youth. But aside from the physical, there are social codes of conduct, practices and expectations that seem to multiply the older you get, especially as a parent.

It was my son that actually got me in to skateboarding. I could see the fun that he was having at the park and as I was constantly down there, keeping my eye on him, I thought why not have a go myself? The only way to join this club is to participate. I bought a cruiser and spent the first year just pushing around on the flat ground, finding my balance. When I say finding my balance, I mean both physically, in terms of trying not to fall off my board, and socially.

How would those using the park react to a middle aged man sharing common space with people much younger than them? Oddly enough, no one at the skatepark seemed bothered when I first showed up. All I ever got was encouragement from those around me. Age, it seemed didn't matter to skaters.
I expect that the few parents and grandparents sitting on the park benches watching their offspring (like I used to do) might have had other ideas though. But then again, I'm a man and it's here that my experience differs greatly from Esther's.

ES: Anyone can participate and having a go, being committed and persevering is the route to inclusion. There is so much support for anyone who has a go. The level of support and encouragement is mind blowing, but I get dropped jaws from kids who see me and stare. I must look like their teacher or their mum or grandma! What they see does not compute with their world view where older women look after them. A four year old at Hackney bumps watched me intently through the fence and then said: "I didn't know mummies can do that." I love that I'm spinning the usual order of things on its head. Social expectations anticipate that older adults and particularly mothers with children should not get involved with action sports, danger or risk. As Spowart and Burrows (2016) remark in their work on snowboarding mothers, 'tensions exist between the identities of a "mother" and the risks often associated with participating in action sports'.

Whilst we have much in the way of shared experience in learning to skate later in life, it's not until Esther brings up the notion of parental roles that I begin to think that I might have an easier ride. Dads riding a skateboard, well that might appear childish (grow up!), or maybe even gung-ho, but mums clearly face challenges that most men don't encounter.

Back in the park, I found that other skaters were more than willing to share their knowledge and were stoked when they could see I was making progress. The teenagers became teachers.

ES: My 13 year old son has become very good at psyching me into things. He'll say, when I stall over something I could do the day before, "mum the ramp hasn't changed, you've done this, you've got this." We started learning together and he is now way ahead, but amazingly still likes to skate with me every now and again.

This makes me chuckle as I can recount very similar scenes with my own son. There was a period of a year or so back where I found myself at my local Hyde Park in Leeds, standing around with a bunch of other dads, bemoaning the fact that our kids don't want to come skating with us anymore. It brings to mind Esther's comments about the radical element of people learning to skate later in life, It's radical because we are doing it for the first time, unlike other adults returning to skating after a hiatus, and that brings with it an advantage. We are free of the feeling that we can no longer do the things that we used to be able to do. I often encounter, both IRL and through watching clips, parts and in written media, veteran skaters who lament their shrinking trick portfolios. This is in direct contrast to our experience, where every bit of progress is simply that, progress. It's an achievement, something new.

ES: Sure, but our progress, particularly at our age, is metered by the possibility of injury, the risk, must be outweighed by the potential gain. Arguably, the social and psychological health benefits from skating and especially gaining a new trick (your never ending beer glass) are greater than the risk presented by another 'swellbow' or similar. A sedentary, risk averse lifestyle would be potentially more destructive to health in the long run. Rodney Mullen [a professional skater in his late fifties] talks of 'cognitive override' in one of his TED talks (Oct 2013). He describes the situation, where 'every fibre of your being says don't do that again', but skaters get up and the cognitive override kicks in.

I think this goes some way towards explaining why, certainly for me, that the progress appears much slower when compared to that of my son. That cognitive override is inhibited by the knowledge that my ageing body takes longer to heal.

ES: *To engage in skateboarding I have to overrule social expectations and find a balance between risk, skill and the sub conscious. To find the tipping point that occurs after learning the skills to do something. This is when I have to stop thinking about it and let my body take over. Trust that I know what to do, feel it: not think it. There is an enormous need to trust in your skills and let yourself be out of control, to embrace that feeling and enjoy it. To allow the body to take over from the mind. As an adult learner, this is difficult to do as we have learned to try and control everything.*

Learning by trial and error, as my son and 10 year old daughter do, is too risky for me. Being in a good physical state is important. I take longer to recover from injury, so I am more cautious than a child. As an expert professional I need to be a learner again. To be shit at it and know nothing, to learn from my children and their friends. This allowed me to re-evaluate learning and explore through my own experience, through my body. The learner/teacher dynamic is fascinating in the skatepark, I'm interested in reciprocal exchange that takes place as part of critical pedagogy - a political act that empowers rather than stultifies the learner.

But why now, especially given what you've just said about the risks involved, why learn to skateboard in your late forties?

ES: *There are loads of reasons why now is the 'right' age for me to learn to skate. As a young woman I was way too self conscious to fail publicly and to look like a dick. Now I have the confidence of an older established woman. I'm not looking to impress or find a boyfriend. I am kind of free from some of the things that would have made me self-conscious. I'd made quite a few big steps forward in my life, buying a house, having kids, getting a PhD. Those progressions had been achieved, and new challenges or life moments had slowed up. Then along came skateboarding and I could keep growing and changing rather than settle into contented middle-age. I didn't want to stop developing, evolving.*

That's punk. That notion of just doing something, getting up and having a go, regardless of what others might think. I like that. For me there is a similarity in the idea present at the dawn of the punk era in the mid/late 70s. That anyone could get up on stage and form a band, *'this is a chord, this is another, this is a third - now form a band'.* In many ways this translates into my own experience of first stepping on a board. By doing so I joined a band, it felt like I'd come home. There's also a huge Do It Yourself culture and artistic creativity among skateboarders and this appeals to me greatly, particularly vis-a-vis corporate behemoths and the 'olympicisation' of skateboarding itself. Progressing on my board and learning new stuff, most recently getting backside slashes, feels like I used to when I added another 7 inch single to my record collection. It somehow legitimises my position as a skateboarder.

ES: *Also, that idea of 'skill sharing' - the idea that knowledge is something to be shared collaboratively, not 'held' by experts and dispensed to the masses. This is a punk idea and one that is very much in play in the pedagogy of the skatepark. It's where the regulation and calibration that will happen as part of skateboarding's inclusion in the Olympics, SLS and other big competitions worries me. What we learn and when we learn it is up to us, and our bodies. It's not part of a syllabus, we don't have to follow a set route and there is no all-knowing 'teacher' figure who will judge us.*

For me learning a new trick brings an enormous sense of reward. It's like acquiring something new. I think about this as an alternative or resistance to capitalist consumer culture. I feel that the reward and the acquisition of a new trick as a thing, it's something I have, something I own but has no commercial value. The satisfaction is like a new pair of shoes but much better. I don't need to acquire goods when I can acquire new learns. I guess this is part of the punk DiY, do it for free, resist ideology that I and you I expect were acculturated with as youths.

Esther is right about that. I was brought up to question authority, don't always assume that those in charge actually know what they are doing. By taking up skating in my fifties I feel that I am challenging the norm, so when the miserable chap in his car tells me to grow up, I just push harder, faster, looking for the next challenge (front side slash grinds)

ES: *I really like this notion of how skateboarding is seen by older people in society. This rocking of the natural order of things makes some people uncomfortable. It's taken me a while to realise their reaction most often is about them and not actually about me. I shouldn't internalise their vibe. The discomfort that my skating produces in others is theirs to deal with. I just ride on. The feeling of rolling removes the block that comes from feeling self conscious, conspicuous. My skating is seen negatively as showing off by some of my peers. Too right I'm showing off! It's a hard won skill. I don't make much art for exhibitions these days, instead I skate, and this involves my body. But I'm not showing off my body, I'm showing off what I can do with it. Celebrating being able to (still).*

My conversation with Esther and others like her is ongoing. I was heartened and in a way not really surprised to find that we share certain elements and experiences. I feel that to admit to a bit of showing off legitimises our experience, it reaffirms all the other elements of enjoyment we gain, while at the same time it provides a platform, or rather a label, a mechanism by which our detractors are able to make sense of our behaviour. "Grow up!".

SKATEBOARDING & NUTRITION
FEED YOUR HEAD

Having made my way as a food writer for the past decade or so, It occurred to me that food is intrinsic to a skater's capacity to perform. Every single indoor skatepark I have visited in the UK has some form of cafe, usually offering a range of deep fried carbohydrate. I've long since had the desire to become the Jay Rayner of the skate kitchen restaurant. I'm not sure I would manage to squeeze a contract with a broadsheet, but look out for a column called 'Stale Fish - No Chips' in a skate mag coming soon.

The idea of throwing recipes into a book about skateboarding came from my time as a volunteer with SkatePal in Palestine. I was out there for two weeks back in 2018, staying in a village just north of Nablus called Asira Al-Shamalia. While there we volunteers were often invited to dine with families in their homes or parents would show up at the skatepark with bags of home-cooked food for us to take back to our apartment to eat. We also spent a good deal of time up at Abood's felafel shop. My experience in Palestine began to cement the relationship between skateboarding and the kitchen. Eating local food is very much part of the experience of being a volunteer for such programmes. Lisa Jacob, a volunteer with Concrete Jungle Foundation captured the sentiment in her 2019 Zine, Out of the Blues,

"we share the food, the floor, the sweat, the fear, the pain, the excitement, the relief, the love, everything…" (Jacob: 2019).

Discovering new treats rapidly became part of the story for me in Palestine, part of the whole vibe of being there, evoking future memories, recalling time and place. My first taste of Knafe, for example, felt like an inauguration to the SkatePal family as I stood in a narrow back street in the old city of Nablus shovelling plastic spoonfuls of the classic sweet pastry into my mouth. It's a ritual that almost every SkatePal volunteer undergoes, and they rave about Knafe, even if they don't actually like the stuff.

All of the ingredients for the amazing food that parents brought to the skatepark in Asira were available from grocers and stores in the village, and as a food writer, it made sense to document this. I wandered the streets, taking notes and making pictures. On my return from volunteering with SkatePal, I put together and self published a small book. It contained twenty-five recipes, all inspired by ingredients readily available. CookPal (Red Fez Books: 2018) ran to three print runs and sold nigh-on five hundred copies in a matter of weeks, with half the profits going to the charity that had provided me with the opportunity in the first place. smörgåsBOARD builds on this idea and celebrates the fact that the sharing of good food goes hand in hand (or possibly served in the same bowl) with skateboarding.

"Over the years I've travelled around Europe and two things have been a constant feature on my trips: Skateboarding and kebab. Whether I was in Istanbul or East Berlin ... the post-skate pilgrimage to the kebab shop has always been the go-to option."

(Jack Bellamy: Döner, 2019)

As a teenager, I took Home Economics at school, I managed a grade 3 CSE. I'll never forget the look on Mrs Walker's face when I told her I was cooking deep-fried egg and chips for my exam practical, it was the kind of expression you see on your dad's face when you tell him you've just been busted for shoplifting - utter disappointment. Having managed to convince her that deep frying was a precise skill, I was allowed to proceed, but sadly I lacked the precise skill required and managed to burn my chips.

Sadly I've no idea of what happened to Mrs Walker and the class of '82, but I do know that I owe this teacher a debt of gratitude for leaving me with a love of food, cooking, eating and writing about it. Skateboarding and food can be seen to go hand in hand in another interesting way, there's commonality in the vernacular; carving, shredding, grinding, boneless, roastbeef, stalefish, salad and bean plant of course (all terms for an array of skateboard tricks or moves). I get stoked on skateing a bowl, especially at a jam. Spread it thick.

Skateboarding is a high-energy activity, it places huge physical demands on the body and many of those demands must be met with a diet that suits their needs. Yeh yeh yeh, blah, blah blah, try telling that to your younger self. As a 'later skater' I'm constantly wondering about the effect that skateboarding is having on my ageing body. Having been lucky enough so far not to have snapped an ulna or a radius, you could say I'm either not skating hard enough, or that my calcium and vitamin D intake over the years have stood me in good stead, and that's probably as a result of never having lived in a shared skate-house. I've heard tales of skate-house kitchen capers that would have made Bourdain gag. Skate capers? Wait a minute, there's a recipe for that:

Recipe for Skate, capers & lemon

Dust a pair of skate wings in seasoned flour and fry gently in butter on both sides. Remove from the pan and set aside. Add another knob of butter to the pan and gently fry a couple of tablespoons of capers, seasoning with a little black pepper and add-in the juice of a lemon. Pour the dressing over the skate and devour.

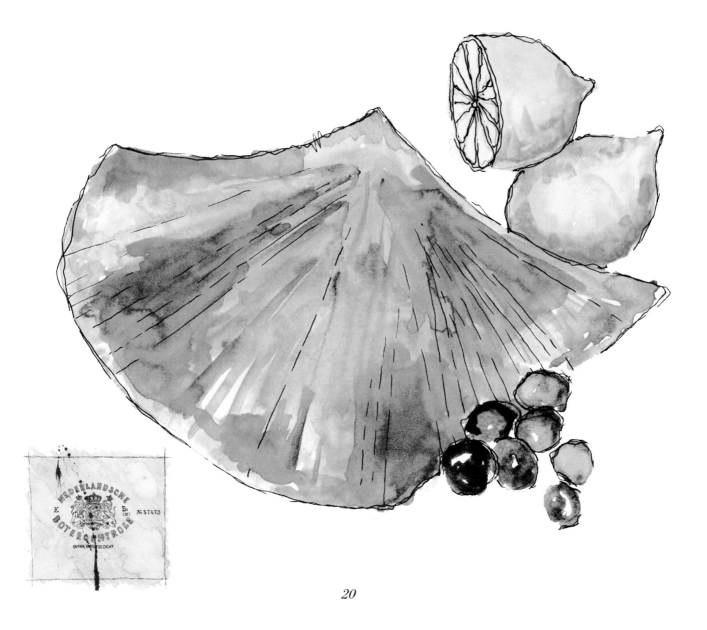

So I never lived in a shared skate-house, but thanks to an anecdote told often by a good pal, I can tell you there's fun to be had by spending an hour or two colouring grains of rice black with a felt pen, snarfing all the biscuits in the house and scattering said blackened grains in the cupboard, then blaming it on the mice! Try it, but don't forget to shred the packet so it looks like it's been gnawed.

Clearly skaters come in all shapes, sizes, genders and ages and each of those 'categories' bring with them particular nutritional requirements. Different styles of skating demand differing quantities of proteins, carbohydrates and minerals. A gentle push around flat ground takes way less energy than a full-on vert session or an entire morning learning kick flip to manual. Those requirements also change as we grow older and we slowly realise that we no longer bounce as easily as we used to.

Skateboarders are not traditionally known for their dietary integrity. A diet of pizza and energy drinks, or chronic and booze, will have a limiting effect on any athlete's capacity to perform, but change seems afoot out there. Chronic! There's a word I learned recently, we used to call it dope in my day, red leb, soap bar, gold seal 'rocky' and 'home grown' - to be avoided on account of its poor quality. It's skater slang for weed.

It's no coincidence that in practically every indoor skatepark, certainly in Britain at least, there is a cafe of some sort usually proffering a menu of fried carbohydrate in the form of chips. I could do a nice deep-fried egg with that if you like. Rock-up at The House of Vans in London (now sadly closed) however, or Spit and Sawdust in Cardiff or Graystones up in Manchester, and you'll find a menu for the more discerning palate, in fact you might even have to phone ahead to book a table. Here you'll find vegetarian and vegan options, salads and felafel.

It's not just carb-fuelled energy that skaters need. Protein aids growth, muscle development and tissue repair, vitamin C is essential in facilitating skin repair and calcium is needed for healthy bones, which will help mitigate fracture, but perhaps the most useful of all nutrients is vitamin K, which aids the clotting of blood! There's always blood.

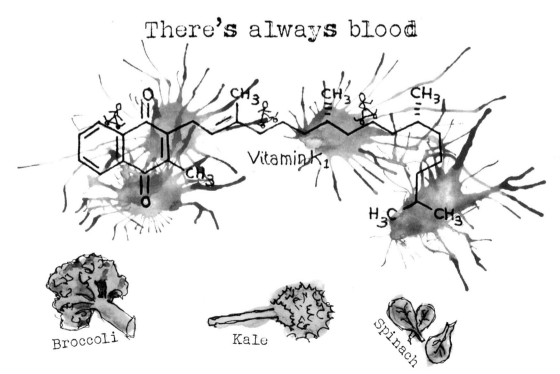

There's always blood

Vitamin K_1

Broccoli   Kale   Spinach

Matt Beare is someone who knows a thing or two about nutrition, he set up *The Daily Push*, a website offering nutritional advice to skateboarders. I caught up with him via email:

When did you set up The Daily Push and why?

The first thought of The Daily Push came around 2016, a few months after my body completely shut down and I thought I wasn't gunna be able to skate again - I herniated 2 discs in my back popping a frontside flip on flat, had patella tendonitis, and a hip problem that ended up needing surgery. It hit me during my year of recovery and no skating that if I knew more about health and how to take better care of myself, I probably could have avoided these issues and time off my board. The Daily Push really started from just wanting to help other skaters avoid unnecessary time off their board, even though now it's evolved to cover a load more topics like performance hacks that enhance how we skate and to destroy the idea that feeling haggard at twenty five is normal!

How did you learn about nutrition? Are you self-taught?

For the first couple of years whilst I was preparing the website I was just self-taught, I hit the books hard for hours every day trying to learn as much on my own as I could, but I was still seriously under-qualified for the job haha. I then decided I needed some qualifications and studied to become a personal trainer with the NSCA and nutrition with Precision Nutrition. At the end of the day though I learnt the most through actually working directly with skaters.

Your website carries some pretty detailed information and advice about what goes on in our bodies at an almost molecular level, What THREE words would you use as best advice for a healthy skate-life?

This question's hard - I was gunna leave that as my 3 words, but I guess I'll go for - Sleep, recover & listentoyourbody (does that count as one word?).

Any plans for a book in the near future?

Actually yes! Even though I've been slacking hard on finishing it recently. I've got about 85% of a book on skate recovery written – recovery being between session recovery and how you adapt to skating – not recovering from injuries. The thing is though, with recovery how you live in general and what you do in the twenty one hours you're not skating is a thousand times more important than what you do in the hour after you skate. So it's turned out to be more of a guide on just how to keep your body as prepared and on point for skating as possible and easy ways to blend living healthy with a skate lifestyle. Hopefully I'll finish it soon!

Matt's website is packed with accessible info down to a micro-biological level with a healthy dose of humour thrown in to boot. Humour always helps.

FEED YOUR HEAD

Humour, our state of mind, is important. Just as we take-on nutrients to aid and maintain our physical health and keep skating, skating in turn nourishes our minds. It plays a huge role in maintaining our mental health as well as that of our physical bodies. Paul O'Connor writes in his fascinating book *Skateboarding and Religion (Palgrave Macmillan: 2020)*, 'Skateboarding provides a meditation, a sense of community, a feeling of power and self-determination', and this idea is often encapsulated in the somewhat clichéd mantra 'skateboarding saved my life'. A number of skateboarders, both professional and amateur alike have written or spoken, detailing their struggles with mental health and finding a degree of salvation through skateboarding. Rodney Mullen talks of how skateboarding would pull him from a 'quagmire of depression' *(The Mutt: Day St. 2004),* Former Pro Skaters Jim Bates and John Rattray have spoken out about their own ordeals. Similar stories can be found the world over in books, blogs and interviews in skateboarding media, but what is it about skateboarding that, for some, has the capacity to bring someone back from the edge?

Skateboarding GB recently released findings, from what amounts to a feel good report, that found 'a striking correlation between people who skateboard and their improved mental health'. The report was undertaken by Instinct Laboratory, a market research company, and Flo Skatepark in Nottingham. It goes on to describe how some people use skateboarding as a coping mechanism for their emotions. Whilst more rigorous and tested research remains within the realm of academe, most certainly from my own experience, the correlation between skateboarding and mental well-being is clear and was amplified by the abstinence enforced by the first lockdown in 2020. The endorphin rush alone, as I dropped-in the mini at Hyde Park once again following the first lifting, was enough to wash away the pent-up frustration of being cooped-up for weeks.

Whilst skateboarding may have a positive effect on the mental health for many of those who do it, sadly it is not a magic panacea. The tragedy of a number of high-profile skaters in recent years having taken their own lives is testament to that, but such devastating events have highlighted the issue of mental health and brought it much more out into the open. Initiatives like the *It's okay project* and *The Ben Raemers Foundation* have emerged from the skateboarding scene to prompt conversation and open-up a dialogue, not just among skaters, but among a broader cross-section of society. In a world which has been affected most recently by the current pandemic and the necessity of lockdown - to the extent that logic and proportion have fallen sloppy dead, we would all do well to remember what the dormouse said, feed your head, feed your head, FEED YOUR HEAD!

THE RISE OF THE SOCIAL SKATE MOVEMENT

The rise of what might be called the international social skate movement has helped develop skateboarding in communities, worldwide. In 2008, Oliver Percovich, an Australian skater, founded Skateistan in Kabul, the capital of Afghanistan. Skateistan and the many other social skate projects around the world have opened up skateboarding to communities in countries often affected by war or civil disruption, places where children and young people lack safe spaces in which to grow, play and develop.

The Skate-Aid scene, or international Social Skate movement to give it a less patronising and imperialistic title in my view, has flourished in recent years. When I say flourished, of course, I mean that the numbers of projects has increased. The projects themselves are constantly on the lookout for funding sources and rely almost entirely on volunteers. Current figures indicate that there are some one hundred and twenty four projects working in over fifty five different countries*. The notion of skaters 'wanting to give something back' is one that goes hand in hand with skateboarding itself. That 'inclusive' element noted in the introduction, as skaters are often keen to share their expertise among themselves, is most certainly one of the elements which drive today's Social Skate movement. This philanthropic element of skateboarding is most easily recognised in the form of the foundations and projects set up by professional skaters, often extremely wealthy ones at that.

*www.goodpush.org

Tony Hawk, for example, perhaps the most famous of professional skaters, set up the Tony Hawk Foundation (now called The Skatepark Project) in 2008. Rob Dyrdek and Ryan Shekler are also former professional skaters who established philanthropic foundations to aid and support healthy communities by promoting skateboarding. There are many others. The rise of the international Social Skate movement, far from being set-up by millionaires, appears as what might be seen as a grass-roots response to the philanthropic urge of the skateboarder. Whereas the likes of Hawk et al have clearly benefitted financially, earning millions of dollars from their 'craft', and are clearly keen to 'put something back' through the excellent work of their respective foundations, the pioneers of the Social Skate movement are responding to the urge without the benefit of a healthy personal bank balance. Volunteers raise their own funds to cover their expenses.

Former pro-skater, now professor of architectural history at the University of Oregon, Ocean Howell once described skaters as 'the shock-troops of gentrification'. He was writing about a public plaza in Philadelphia, known as Love Park. The plaza was built in the mid 1960s as public open space, but by the late 1980s it had become increasingly used by the homeless population of the city as a place to sleep and hang out during the day. Consequently it was seen by the public as a 'no-go area'. It was deemed unsafe. By the end of the 1980s however, skateboarders had begun to gravitate towards the plaza, which offered a number of interesting and challenging obstacles for skating. It's amazing just how far the call of a granite ledge will travel, attracting street skaters from miles around.

As more and more skaters began to use the park, they were increasingly seen by the public as 'tempering the activities of the homeless population' (Howell: 2005) and the public began to feel safe using the park, as it once again became an asset to the city. Despite the apparent positive outcome of skaters moving in to Love Park, the city authorities chose to re-design the park in the early 2000s and effectively excluded the skater population ahead of a broader gentrification project of the whole area. In effect, the 'shock troop' skaterswere 'sent-in' (or rather tolerated for a while by the authorities) to clear out the 'undesirables' (i.e. homeless population) and were then, in turn, excluded to make way for the 'generals' and their capitalist victory parade as the area was developed. Playing with this idea a little, and substituting the notion of 'positive change' for the word gentrification, I believe that Howell's observations can, to a degree, be applied to much of the Social Skate movement.

That is to say that, where these organisations move in, then positive change is sure to follow. The difference is that, while in the case of Love Park, the 'positive change' which followed was to the detriment of the skaters themselves, when it comes to volunteering for such a project, then the skaters as well as the locals enjoy a lasting benefit. That benefit continues as volunteers return from their adventures and 'share the stoke' with others, some of whom are keen to get involved and volunteer in their own right.

From my own perspective, just as the citizens of Philadelphia were reluctant to enter Love Park on account of a perceived danger, I too have been reluctant to visit countries like Angola, Afghanistan and Syria on account of a perceived danger held by a significant number of the world's population. But thanks to the efforts of organisations like *Concrete Jungle Foundation*, *SkatePal*, *Skateistan* and *Skate-Aid*, and the skaters that volunteer for them, I feel more confident in visiting these places and can also enjoy the benefits of positive change.

Whilst individual Social Skate projects may operate in different ways, each adapting to the political and social/religious environment in which they work, the stories of how these projects came about often share a degree of similarity. The majority are set up by skaters, often a single individual who, for whatever reason, found themselves abroad with their skateboard and enjoyed a positive reaction from the local population. Children, not familiar with skateboarding, proved curious and keen 'to have a go'. Charlie Davis, founder and Director of *SkatePal*, describes the excitement of the local kids as a factor in his decision to set up a skateboarding project in Palestine.

"I took my board out with me on my first trip and saw how excited the kids were, as they'd never seen [a skateboard] before. From that point I knew that skateboarding would take off."

SkatePal Magazine, Issue 1, 2017

Similarly Oliver Percovich, prior to setting-up Skateistan, recounts a familiar story of arriving in Afghanistan with his skateboard and attracting the attention of local children,

"One of the really special memories for me was a time that the girls at the fountain [a plaza in Kabul] held hands and started to dance around I couldn't believe what I was seeing - the penny dropped, this can't just stop here. It can't just be these little skateboard sessions in the street, this has the ability to unite people from very very different backgrounds ... It gave me concrete proof that skateboarding is this great way of connecting people together."

Interview in Skateism Magazine, Issue 2, June 2018.

These stories are significant, and play an important role in attracting volunteers (like myself) as well as funding. Writing in the Journal of Sport and Social Issues (2013), academics, Holly Thorpe and Robert Rinehart pick up on the significance of 'origination stories'. Their joint paper examines the role and function of action sport NGOs in a Neoliberal context and in it they suggest that organisations like Skateistan produce 'carefully constructed "origination stories" that focus on the personal journey of a key individual.' It's a tactic that works well and can serve as a useful 'hook' when seeking to attract newspaper copy and exposure as it always makes for interesting reading. But it is also useful when it comes to attracting volunteers to work for a project. Certainly in my own case when I first volunteered for SkatePal, even though by the time that I arrived in Palestine the organisation had been operating for five years, I felt that on an individual level, I too was sharing in Charlie Davis' original stoke. Once I got to the village of Asira Al Shamalia, where I was to be volunteering, a whole load of other factors came in to play, which made for an unforgettable experience.

One of the many challenges that Non Governmental Organisations (NGOs), such as *Skateistan*, *Concrete Jungle Foundation*, *SkatePal*, and others, face is the accusation of cultural imperialism. This is the idea that these NGOs are forcing western ideals upon cultures where they do not traditionally exist. Whilst those that volunteer for such projects (as well as the organisations themselves) might refute such accusations, it can be increasingly difficult for them to do so, particularly where these organisations are working in politically sensitive areas. The need for the NGOs to maintain a positive, or at best neutral, relationship with the authorities in which they operate is paramount. Those 'authorities' of course also include the parents and relatives of the children attending. *Skateistan*, for example, has enjoyed a deal of publicity in western media in recent years; *Skateboarding in Afghanistan Provides a Diversion From Desolation* (New York Times: 2009), *Skateboarding Makes Afghan Girls Feel Free* (Vice: 2015), *Skategirls of Kabul - in pictures* (Guardian: 2015). But founder, Oliver Percovich is keen to stress that Western influences, such as music and fashion are not part of the *Skateistan* programme. Interviewed in 2011, Percovich explained that were the children seen to be taking western cultural cues, then they would be stopped from attending the programme very quickly (Thorpe & Rhinehart: 2013).

TLED BY **TAYBEH BREWING Co.** **TAY**

In my own experience as a volunteer with SkatePal, the volunteer's handbook set out the importance of moderating our dress sense (keep your shirt on while skating boys!), and to respect local alcohol bans. Of course when it comes to alcohol, some skaters and volunteers will go to great lengths to maintain supplies, even in 'dry towns and villages'.

"I don't really remember Agadir. To me it's just where I landed in Morocco and from where I left the country. And also from where all of us were getting drink supplies on the build. Taghazout is a dry town. You're not allowed to drink and there's not a single shop where you can find booze. It was like a rehab centre in which everyone was cheating, especially the Belgians, taking cabs to Agadir on a daily basis just to shop at the supermarket."

Make Life Skate Life volunteer, Lisa Jacob; in, 'Out of the Blues' 2019

For all the arguments about cultural imperialism, and I have paid close attention to many of them in researching this book, largely because I can't bare the idea that I'm some kind of ageing skateboarding imperialist do-gooder, I'm of a mind that it is the inclusivity of skateboarding, the willingness to share the stoke, that beats at the heart of the Social Skate movement. It's not so much that volunteers are exporting some exclusively western cultural value, there is no big agenda, they are not selling anything per se. Sure, volunteers get a lot out of the experience, travelling to foreign lands and experiencing foreign food and cultures, but equally the locals with whom they build parks and skate, gain novel experiences too. This is born of my own experience in visiting some of the projects and countries represented in this book. In Palestine I was struck by what I saw as a mutual exchange as parents brought food to share at Rosa skate park in Asira. Just as we encouraged youngsters to have a go at skateboarding, we in turn were encouraged to try new foods and to learn a few words of a foreign language. In the end, I don't really have a problem with the notion of cultural imperialism, I don't see that it applies in this case. As far as I can see the international Social Skate movement spreads enjoyment and surely enjoyment is not specific to any one culture in particular.

One of the things I did struggle with, and that was while volunteering in Palestine, is the political environment in which I was volunteering. I found it frustrating that while witnessing large scale abuses of human rights and the wholly unjust treatment of Palestinians as a whole by the state of Israel, we are asked as volunteers not to 'rock the boat' in any political sense. The reasons why are obvious and plain to see, it would be easy for the Israeli authorities to shut down the programme. So perhaps in this case, this is where the problem of cultural imperialism lies, and not with the volunteers who after all just wanna skate.

PALESTINE & MY SKATEPAL EXPERIENCE

In October 2018, just over a year after I started skateboarding, I traveled to Palestine as a one time volunteer with SkatePal. Based in the village of Asira Al Shamalia, just north of Nablus, I found myself teaching the rudiments of skateboarding to Palestinian children, as well as a growing number of enthusiastic parents and on the odd occasion, grandparent who were actually my age. As volunteers at the skatepark, we were welcomed with smiling eager faces from the children, and with copious amounts of home cooked food brought along by parents to share with us.

As I flew in to Tel Aviv at night, with the city lights spread out below me, my mind jumped back almost thirty years to 1989, when I first landed at Ben Gurion airport. Back then I was in my early twenties, carrying little more than a Swiss army knife, a guitar and an undeclared consignment of the confidence of youth. Arriving in 2018, just two days before my 53rd birthday, and having swapped my guitar for a skateboard, I retraced the journey made some three decades before. I took a bus straight to Jerusalem, Al Quds - to give it it's original Arabic name. I spent the night in a hostel in the old city, before heading for the bus station outside the Damascus gate, and hopping on a bus to Ramallah the next morning. Back in '89 as I sat on the rooftop terrace of the hostel looking over the city, I remember being struck, not by the religious significance of Jerusalem to muslims, christians and jews alike, but by a sense of adventure probably best summed up by the antics of Indiana Jones and his insatiable sense of derring-do. I distinctly remember the theme tune of that iconic film rattling through my young head at the time. It came as little surprise, almost thirty years later, that on my second visit to this magnificent city, once again the opening bars of John Williams' theme tune to Raiders of the Lost Ark, ran through my mind, only this time they were amplified by my own sense of derring-do and adventures to come.

The sights and smells emanating from cafes, restaurants and spice stalls throughout the old city remind the visitor that many modern cookbooks owe their origins to the Middle East. Ancient Mesopotamian recipes have been found carved in tablet form and date from 1700BC. More recently, *The Book of Dishes* (Kitaab al-Tabikh) dates from the thirteenth century. Written by Muhammad b. al-Hassan b. Muhammad b. al-Karim, the scribe of Baghdad, it was for centuries the favourite cookery book of the Ottoman Empire. The original remains to this day in the Suleymaniye Library in Istanbul. It's impossible to visit the Middle East without thinking about food, it's as if the entire region is built around it.

Author of the definitive, *A New Book of Middle Eastern Food* (first published in 1968), Claudia Roden, notes '*that an interest in Middle Eastern cuisine has mirrored the relationship between Europe and the followers of Islam, and that Middle Eastern Food has had the greatest impact on cooking in Europe.*'

Many of the culinary terms and names for ingredients we use in the kitchen have their origins in the Middle East, coffee comes from *qahwah*, saffron *za'faran*, sherbert from *shariba,* meaning to drink, which also gives up *syrup*. New ingredients, such as sumac and Dukkah seem to find their way into western supermarkets on a daily basis. There is certainly something to be said for wandering around the food markets in the old city. It brings you up close with where our food comes from. The sight of offal or freshly plucked chickens, hanging in front of a stall seems to me to be a much more honest approach to our dominance of the food chain. As supermarkets have extended their control over the food supply the world over in recent years, we've seen a 'sanitisation' of eating meat and poultry. Clean cuts of meat, and plump plucked chickens, wrapped neatly in plastic give little honest clue as to what the beast once looked like, or how it might have been raised.

At home in our supermarkets, we are bombarded with weasel words insisting that animals are 'raised with care by farmers who share our values'. It's an attempt to placate a growing consumer concern for the welfare of livestock. In the age of the factory farm, where livestock is raised as quickly and economically as possible in order to extract maximum profit, perhaps it would be an idea to do away with the notion of 'farm' altogether and just stick with the word factory. I am convinced that if we knew a little more about how our meat and poultry is actually raised and slaughtered, then we all might eat a little less, if not give it up altogether, and from an environmental perspective alone, that would be no bad thing.

It seems that the stalls in the markets, or souks, of the old city of Jerusalem are arranged by whatever it is that vendors are selling. So you are likely to find that all the butchers will be grouped together in a particular area of the souk, and likewise the fishmongers and grocers. This system makes a lot of sense, enabling customers to see who has the freshest ingredients and make a choice as who to buy from. While some visitors might find it difficult or distasteful walking through the meat market on account of the hanging carcasses on display, the other tremendous advantage to this system where vendors are grouped according to produce, is that by the time you get to the spice market, then olfactory senses are besieged by aromas absent from your average supermarket. Food shopping by smell, as well as appearance, of ingredients is very much the way to do it here.

Food played a vital role in our relationships with the villagers of Asira, not least because we were constantly invited into peoples' homes to sit down and eat with them. We were plied with tubs of hummus, stuffed green peppers and courgettes, fresh rolled kibbe and all manner of treats. It was actually while sitting in the home of a local family, watching mother roll seasoned lamb mince and cooked rice in blanched chard leaves to make tiny 'cigars', which would later be baked in a fresh tomato sauce and served up as the family meal after Friday prayers, that I began to realise the connection between the skateboard and the chopping board.

Between the food brought to us at the park by parents and the frequent trips up the hill in Asira to Abood's felafel shop, we hardly cooked at all back in the volunteers' apartment, and like I said earlier, once we discovered knafe I don't think the stove top saw another pot or pan in the two weeks I was out there.

SHAKSHUKA

Ingredients:

A little olive oil
1 Onion (finely chopped)
1 Red pepper (de-seeded and sliced lengthwise)
4 cloves of garlic (finely chopped)
1 tsp of paprika
1 tsp ground cumin
1 Tin of chopped tomatoes
2 eggs
Sea salt & fresh ground black pepper
A handful of chopped flat leaf parsley

Gently fry the chopped onion in the olive oil. When the onion begins to take on some colour, throw in the chopped garlic, the red pepper, the cumin and the paprika, stir well and simmer gently for a couple of minutes. Add the chopped tomatoes and turn up the heat to reduce the sauce. When the tomato sauce has reduced by about a third, turn down the heat and crack in the eggs and cook for a further five minutes or until the eggs have turned white. Season and sprinkle with chopped flat leaf parsley and serve with bread.

A SIMPLE FLATBREAD

The price of bread is subsidised by the gorvenment in a number of countries in the Middle East. Damascus, for example, is peppered with government bakeries, which open in the morning selling subsidised bread. By midday they are all closed up. It's a means of making sure that people have food in their bellies and are less likely to kick up a fuss. Having said that much of the impetus for the so called 'Arab Spring', which swept across the region in 2010, lay with the increasing price of food and the cost of living under oppressive regimes.

The style and type of bread varies from region to region. The village bakery in Asira Al Shamalia was a regular early morning port of call. If we got there in time and the bakers were still at it, we'd sometimes have a fresh baked flatbread with beaten egg on top. Eggy bread straight from the oven.

Ingredients:

150g plain yoghurt
150g self raising flour
A pinch of salt
A little vegetable oil for cooking

Combine all the ingredients in a bowl to form a soft dough. Knead gently for a couple of minutes and divide the dough evenly into balls (this recipe makes four). Flatten out the balls between your palms and cook in a lightly oiled hot griddle pan for about two or three minutes on each side.

TABOULEH

Ingredients:

250g bulgur wheat
A bunch of fresh mint
A bunch of flat leaf parsley
Half a cucumber
6 spring onions
A few cherry tomatoes (quartered)
Lots of olive oil
Juice of a lemon
Salt & Ground black pepper

Place the bulgur wheat and a pinch of salt in a saucepan and cover with water so that there is about 1cm of water above the wheat. Bring to boil and turn to a very low simmer until the water is absorbed by the wheat. When cooked, the wheat should be white in colour and firm but not crunchy to the bite. Drain the wheat through a sieve and rinse with cold clean water. Drain very well and place in a bowl. While the bulgur wheat is cooking, remove the stalks from the parsley and mint and chop finely. Slice the spring onions and chop the cucumber into small chunks. Quarter the tomatoes and add the lot to the bowl with the cooked wheat. Pour over a few good glugs of top quality olive oil and squeeze the juice of the lemon. Top with a grind of black pepper and mix well. Let it stand for at least fifteen minutes to allow the flavours to develop.

FELAFEL

I tried making these with tinned chickpeas. It just doesn't work as the felafel falls apart as you fry them in the oil. Using dried chickpeas and soaking them overnight is the only way to get results. Refrigerating, them once you have formed the individual felafel balls, helps keep them together. I'd also recommend picking up one of these felafel presses, you'll find one online and they're not expensive.

Ingredients:

100g dried chickpeas
1 small onion (peeled and roughly chopped)
2 cloves of garlic
A small bunch of fresh coriander (30 g)
A small bunch of flat leaf parsley (30g)
1 tsp ground cumin
Salt & Ground black pepper
2 tbsp sesame seeds
Sunflower oil for frying

Soak the chickpeas in water overnight. Drain well and place in a food processor with the rest of the ingredients. Blend to a thick paste. Shape into small balls and flatten slightly. Refrigerate for at least one hour, then deep fry in sunflower oil until golden. Serve in pitta bread with salad, a dollop of hummus and a splash of tahini.

The short time I spent as a volunteer with SkatePal had a massive impact on me. I'd only been skating for just over a year when I came across SkatePal. I first heard about the project via my local skate scene in Leeds. Blinky, who i'd got to know skateing Hyde Park in Headingley, recounted tales of hill bombing through olive groves, an emerging skate scene under military occupation and a generosity of a community welcoming foreign volunteers into their village. I was keen to return to the Middle East.

From 1994 - 1998 I studied for a degree in Arabic at Durham University, and I had lived in Syria for a year in 1995 as part of the course. It was while the old President Assad was still around, Hafez al Asad was still very much in charge and kept a close watch over his citizens (see photo above, this enormous banner was back-lit at night!). Whilst I was never fluent in Arabic, I was confident in the little I knew and was happy to wander off around the old city of Damascus looking for adventures in the souks and workshops found behind the crumbling city walls. I found that with a few words of a foreign language you can open up doors to friendships and discoveries, that otherwise might never happen. Rad, that isn't it.

The discovery of skateboarding and my consequent SkatePal adventure in 2018, re-kindled that curiosity and sense of discovery that had somehow been eroded, but never quashed, in the two decades since my first Syrian adventures. As I said, the language was never my strong point, but I'd grasped enough of it to serve me well. Through studying Arabic I came across authors such as Naguib Mahfouz, who won the Nobel Prize for Literature in 1988. His 'Cairo Trilogy' (1956-1957) follows three generations of an Egyptian family through colonial rule under the Ottomans, to independence and occupation by the British during the second world war. As my interest in the politics of the Middle East grew I discovered Syrian author Zakaria Tamer's tale of the Tiger on the Tenth Day (1978) and saw correlation between political regimes in the region and the behaviour of the zookeeper in the story. But one of the most moving pieces of Arabic literature I came across was Palestinian, Mahmoud Darwish's poem, 'Identity Card' (1964). It's a powerful piece and takes the form of an exhortation from a Palestinian labourer to an Israeli official, perhaps a guard at a checkpoint or a bureaucrat in some vast office in the city. All of these works are available in English translation and I would urge readers to look them out.

MUTABBAL

The deep smokey flavour of this classic Middle Eastern dip is imparted by blackening the skins of the aubergines over a naked flame, or burning them off under a grill. Once blacked all over, cool off under running cold water and peel away and discard the burned skin.

The rest of the hard work is taken care of by the food processor as all the ingredients are blitzed to a pulp. Dont over do it though, as you want a bit of texture, rather than a totally smooth paste. Scoop mouthfuls up with the fresh flat bread.

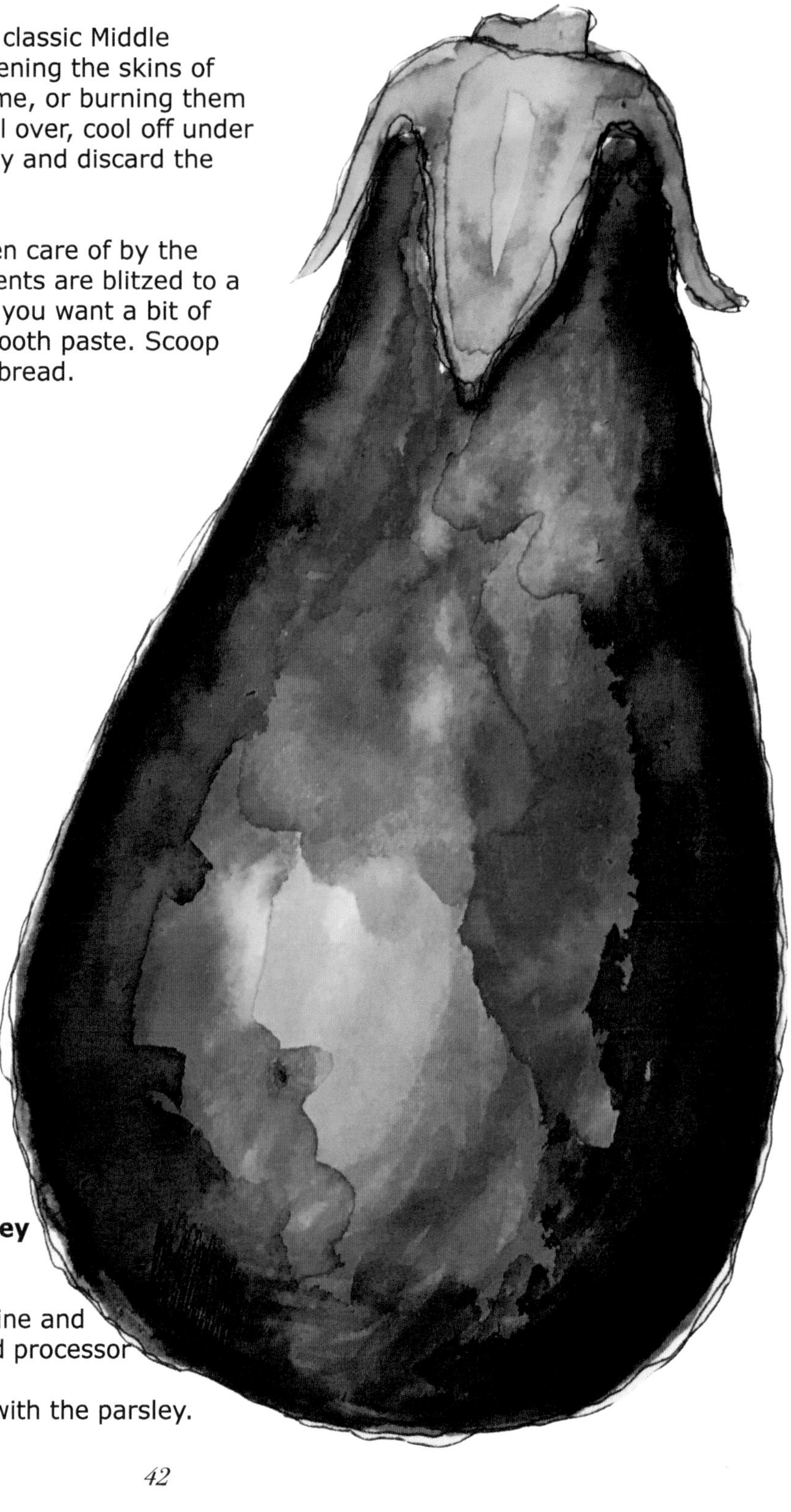

Ingredients:

2 large aubergines
1 tbsp Olive oil
1 clove of garlic
(peeled & chopped)
1 tsp tahini paste
Salt & Black pepper
1 tbsp plain yoghurt
1/4 tsp ground cumin
1 tbsp chopped flat leaf parsley
(For garnish)

Roughly chop the peeled aubergine and bang all the ingredients in a food processor and blitz to a pulp.
Serve in a small bowl sprinkled with the parsley.

cookpal

A Cookbook in Aid of SkatePal

Josh Sutton

HUMMUS

Hummus is the arabic word for chickpeas and if you ask for hummus then that is what you will get. The dip is known as 'hummus bi tahini', it's a staple found all over the middle east and is often offered with flat bread as an appetiser, or a quick snack when you visit someone's house. There's always a bowl of hummus in the fridge.

Purists might argue that hummus should be made with lemon juice, but I use lime juice because I didn't have a lemon one day and used a lime instead, I never went back to lemons.

Ingredients

1 tin of chickpeas (drained)
1 clove garlic (peeled)
4 tbsp olive oil
1 tsp ground cumin
A pinch of salt and fresh
ground black pepper
1 tsp tahini paste
a pinch of dried chilli flakes
juice of half a lime

Place all of the ingredients into a blender and blitz until smooth.

When I returned from Palestine, I gathered my collection of photographs and illustrations and published CookPal, a recipe book, influenced and based on my experience as a SkatePal volunteer. For me, the notion of food and recipes and travel are intrinsically linked. Who doesn't remember the first time they tried 'foreign food' on holiday? One of my favourite ever books is a recipe-based travelogue set in the ancient city of Damascus. Marie Fadel & Rafik Schami's *Damascus, taste of a city* evokes my own memories of living in the oldest continually inhabited city in the world. Even though the book is bereft of photographs, the vivid descriptions of street scenes and recipes instantly transport me back to a *'Street Called Straight'* and the busy hustle of *Souk al Hamidieh*.

The relative success I'd met with the publication of CookPal, two print runs of two hundred and the positive reviews it received, both among the skateboarding community and further afield spurred me on. I was somewhat especially delighted when several of my colleagues in The Guild of Food Writers bought copies and suggested I enter it into the annual awards. It didn't make the shortlist, let alone win! There clearly was something in the idea of a book that combines skateboarding with recipes. I made plans to visit several other international social skate projects, from Jamaica to Jordan and a few places in between but not as a volunteer, just as an observer, to gather ideas for recipes and collect photographs. The opportunity to skate in far flung climes would of course be and added attraction to the project.

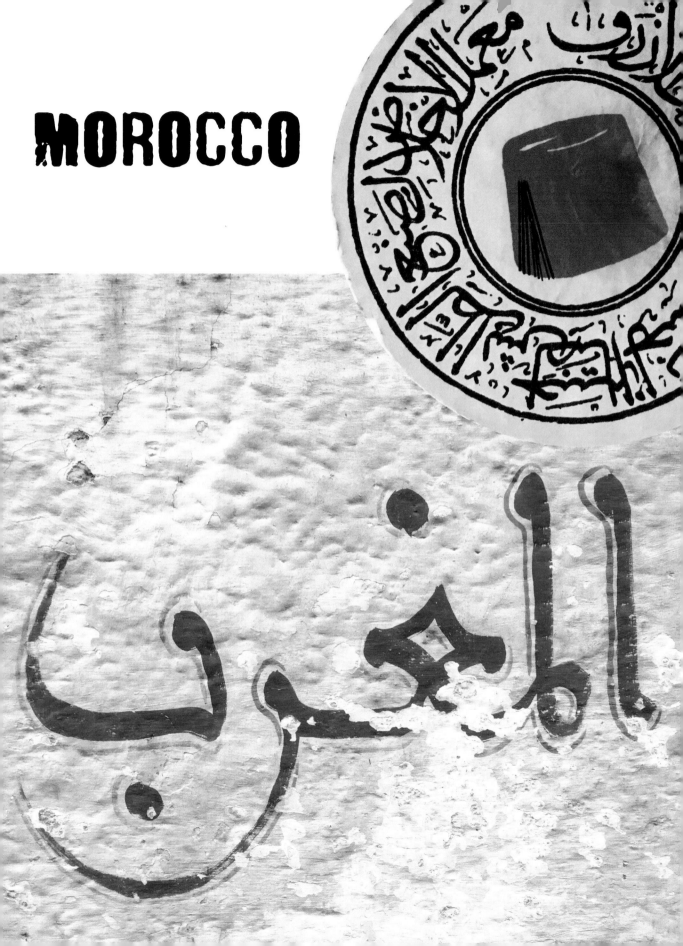

MOROCCO

TAGHAZOUT SKATEPARK

In January 2020 I travelled to Taghazout in southern Morocco. I arrived laden with used decks donated by my local skateshop, *Welcome* in Leeds. Within a couple of hours of handing them over to Ali, a local fixer and self-proclaimed 'President' of the Taghazout Skateboarding Association, the boards were set up and immediately put to use by the local kids. Ali's enthusiasm for the future of the park is seemingly limitless. He diverts some of the profits from his skate shop, in near by Agadir, towards the park at Taghazout. While I was there the beginnings of a garden to the rear of the park were taking shape, the idea being that tall plants and a couple of palm trees might throw some shade over the hottest skatepark in Morocco. It wasn't long before I heard tell of a fish tagine cooking slowly over hot coals.

The connection between food and skating at Taghazout skatepark in Morocco is there for all to see. It's not a nipple, it's a giant tagine lid, slap bang in the middle of the park. Tagine is the thing in Taghazout. Practically every little cafe and restaurant in the village below offers a whole range of tagines on the menu. The park is just outside the village, up a steep hill, just follow the blue arrows.

The park at Taghazout sits atop a hill overlooking the town and out across the Atlantic Ocean. It was built in 2017 by a host of volunteers from all over the globe, working for *Make Life Skate Life*. With funding from Levis Skateboarding, the project took less than three weeks to complete. Lisa Jacob's 'zine '*Out of the Blues*' captures, perfectly, the atmosphere and camaraderie among the volunteers and describes skaters' willingness to share the stoke as an anticapitalist way of thinking,

'For you to win, you have to make everyone else win'·

The notion of skateboarding per se, as an anti-capitalist venture is a tough one to wrestle with, particularly given the financial worth as a global industry, and the fact that Levi's Skateboarding were key investors in the park at Taghazout. But Lisa Jacob's point is focussed solely on the input of the volunteers who came together to build the place, and the fact that people are prepared to work hard for free.

The crew was made up of over 100 men and women of different nationalities from every continent, ranging from 16 to 50 something in age, with different backgrounds, levels of construction experience, and all speaking a big mix of languages. It was the most diverse group of people we'd ever been a part of, yet everyone shared the same passion for skating and building ... There aren't a lot of places where you'll hear a Swedish guy talking to Americans about construction techniques they saw a Japanese woman perform on the jobsite earlier. The sharing of techniques and cultures from around the world is mind blowing in a project like this. From building, skating, spliff rolling, diet, or dice games, we learned a lot from each other.

(McManus & Waldron - Skate Jawn Dec 30th 2018)

And that anti-capitalist sentiment is further reflected in the actions of others who show up later at the park, with equipment to give away.

While at Taghazout, I met Alex Fortin, a Canadian skater who'd spent the past ten years travelling the world checking out skate scenes in the most unlikely places. He'd shown up at Taghazout with half a dozen complete set-ups and donated them to the park and started running free lessons for the locals and anyone else who wanted to join in. He told me he'd dropped 12 completes at a place in Peru the year before.

"It's good to see the kids with 'the skate flame' riding boards they'd otherwise not get their hands on."

Thanks to Alex and the many others that donate equipment, as well as the volunteers who built the place, Taghazout is a place where local kids can show up, borrow a board and shred the park like a pro, or take part in lessons for beginners.

Make Life Skate Life shares a similar origination story with many of the other social skate projects. Founder Arne Hillerns found himself abroad with a board and noticed an inherent curiosity on behalf of the local youth population as he travelled through India, back in 2012. In 2013, after securing sponsorship, MLSL built their first park in India.

Make life skate life.

Since then, together with an international army of volunteers, MLSL have continued to work with grass-roots organisations, building parks across the world from Brazil to Mayanmar. In each case, as the volunteers go their separate ways or move on to the next build, new projects spring up around the new park, offering opportunities to local youth, not just in skateboarding, but often in education and art or informal language classes. It is indeed, these 'legacies' left by social skate projects that underpin the ethos of their creation in the first place.

FISH TAGINE

As soon as Ali got wind of the fact that I was writing a recipe book, he started talking tagine, fish tagine, eel to be precise. Ali had a couple of guys helping out up at the park, and the tagine was cooked by (another) Ali over a small pile of charcoal out the back of the skatepark. The dish bubbled away quietly to itself for the best part of two and a half hours, while chef Ali and his pals continued preparing the land for the small garden that was beginning to take shape and occasionally adding a little more water to the tagine when it got a bit dry.

Ingredients:

Olive oil
2 medium onions (peeled and sliced)
1 small bulb of fennel (chopped)
2 cloves garlic (finely chopped)
1 green pepper (de-seeded and sliced)
1 tsp ground cumin
1 tsp paprika
Salt & Pepper
1 large potato (peeled and sliced)
1 large tomato (sliced)
A large fillet of any white fish (cut into large chunks)
A handful of green olives
300ml fish stock
A bunch of flat leaf parsley
A lemon (cut into wedges)

If you don't have a Tagine, use a high-sided frying pan with a tight fitting lid.

Drizzle some olive oil in the pan and over a medium heat, fry the onions until they begin to colour. Next add the sliced peppers, garlic and chopped fennel, simmer gently for another five minutes and add the cumin and paprika, a good grind of black pepper and a pinch of salt and give it a stir.

Move the ingredients to one side and place a single layer of the sliced potato in the bottom of the pan and cover with the onion and pepper. Place another layer of potato over the top along with the sliced tomato and place the chunks of cod around the pan.

Throw in a handful of olives and pour over the fish stock and half of the chopped parsley (saving the other half for garnish).

Layer on any remaining potato and tomato and place the lid on the pan. Simmer gently for half an hour or until the potato is soft. Garnish with the remaining parsley and a couple of wedges of lemon.

GRILLED FRESH SARDINES

Fresh sardines, cooked on an open fire or over charcoal on the beach, are pretty hard to beat. I don't even bother to gut them, cooking them whole seems to help with keeping them moist and succulent. Three or four fish per person ought suffice, but I have been known to clear off the best part of a dozen in one sitting. The eyes of a fresh fish will still have a bit of sparkle in them, as do mine when I'm eating grilled sardines.

Ingredients:

6 fresh sardines
Olive oil
Flaked sea salt
Juice of lemon

Wash the sardines thoroughly and pat each one dry with kitchen paper.
Drizzle them with olive oil and throw over a good scattering of
flaked sea salt. Grill over hot coals, or under a hot grill,
for three or four minutes on each side.
Drizzle with lemon juice before serving
with a little chopped tomato salad.

I bought a fresh squid from the guy in the white hat here. Inside his little shop he had a conked-out chest freezer full of fresh wet fish, landed that morning. "Fi calamar?" I asked in my broken arabic, is there squid? "Eh! Fi", he said, and sold me a fresh one for 20 dirhams. He didn't even bother to wrap it, just handed it to me in its glorious sticky fresh mess. I didn't quibble about the price, I just grabbed it in my fist, head and tentacles dangling, and took it to the guy next door with the charcoal barbeque. I took a seat at one of the plastic tables and ordered a soda, while the 'chef' cleaned up my 20 dirham squid and cooked it for me over hot coals. Barely five minutes later it was served up on a plate with a little chopped tomato salad and a fresh lime.

57

ROAST CAULIFLOWER & POMEGRANITE SALAD

Ingredients:

1 cauliflower
1 tsp whole cumin seeds
1 tsp fennel seeds
Olive oil
½ tsp dried chilli flakes
3 tbsp pomegranate seeds
2 tbsp pumpkin seeds
1 tsp sumac
Salt & Pepper
Juice of half a lime

Slice the cauliflower, spread out on a baking sheet and drizzle with olive oil and scatter the cumin and fennel seeds over the top. Roast in the oven at 180° C for 40 minutes. Remove to a piece of kitchen roll and allow to cool.

Place the roast cauliflower into a salad bow and add the pomegranate & pumpkin seeds. Drizzle with olive oil and fresh lime juice, scatter over with the sumac and season to taste.

بائع الدجاج والبيض

Vente de Poulets et des Oeufs

06 71 66 80 18

بائع الدجاج

VENDEUR de POULET

CHICKEN SELLER

CHICKEN TAGINE

Ingredients:

6 chicken thighs
Olive oil
1 large onion (peeled and chopped)
2 cloves garlic (peeled and chopped)
2 green peppers (de-seeded and sliced)
1 tin chickpeas (drained)
500ml chicken stock
Salt & Pepper
1 tsp ground cumin
A few strands of saffron

Heat a good glug of olive oil in a Tagine, or a deep sided frying pan. Brown the chicken thighs in the hot oil, remove and set aside. Next, add the chopped onion and fry until it starts to brown then add the chopped garlic and the ground cumin and fry for a further minute. Return the thighs to the pan and add the chickpeas and sliced green pepper along with the saffron and a good grind of black pepper and a pinch of salt. Pour in the chicken stock, place a lid on the tagine/pan and simmer gently for forty minutes. Serve with steamed cous cous.

LAMB STEW WITH CHICKPEAS

Ingredients:

500g Fresh lamb neck fillets
1 large Onion
4 Cloves of garlic
1 Tablespoon of olive oil
1 large Aubergine
Half a bulb of fennel
100g Of fresh root ginger
1 Tin of plum tomatoes
1 Tin of chickpeas
1 Teaspoon Whole Cumin Seeds
2 Tablespoon Whole Coriander seeds
1 Tablespoon Whole fennel seeds
Half a dried red chilli (finely chopped)
Salt & milled black pepper.
Bunch of fresh coriander

Crush the cumin and fennel seeds in a pestle and mortar, and then add the coriander seeds. Grind the lot so the there are no whole seeds remaining. Cut the neck fillets into 2cm chunks and place in a bowl with the crushed seeds. Give it a good mix round with your hand to make sure every piece of meat is coated with the spices.

Finely chop the onion. Heat the olive oil in a large stockpot, add the chopped onion and cook over a low heat until the onion begins to colour. Add the chopped garlic, turn up the heat a little and add the chopped chilli and the meat. Brown the meat on all sides.

Chop the aubergine into 2cm chunks and add this to the stockpot and stir. Turn the heat down and add the tin of tomatoes with a little water, season to taste and cover the pan with a lid. Simmer gently for 30 minutes, stirring occasionally.

Add the drained tin of chickpeas together with the peeled and coarsely grated ginger and the coarsely grated fennel. Cook for a further ten minutes, add the chopped fresh coriander, stir in and remove from heat. Let stand for two or three minutes before serving.

ROAST VEGETABLE COUS COUS

Cous cous needs very little cooking and one of the easiest and quickest ways of preparing cous cous is to soak it in just enough boiling water until it becomes fluffy then season with salt & pepper and fork through a large Knob of butter.

Ingredients:

2 courgettes (roughly chopped)
1 onion (roughly chopped)
1 red onion (roughly chopped)
A whole bulb of garlic (divided into cloves)
2 medium carrots (peeled and cut into sticks)
1 red pepper (de-seeded and sliced)
1 green pepper (de-seeded and sliced)
8 cherry tomatoes
1 tbsp fennel seeds
1 tbsp cumin seeds
300g dried cous cous
A large knob of butter
90ml boiling water
Salt & fresh ground black pepper

Pre-heat the oven to 220°C. Place all of the vegetables plus the seeds into a shallow oven-proof dish. Drizzle with plenty of olive oil and season well with salt & ground black pepper. Stir with a wooden spoon to make sure all the vegetable are coated in olive oil and roast in the hot oven. After 15 minutes, remove the dish and turn the vegetables over with a spatula and replace in the oven for a further 15 minutes, or until the vegetables begin to caramelise.

Once the vegetables are cooked, melt the knob of butter in a large shallow pan and add the dried cous cous. Turn the heat to very low and stir to coat the cous cous in butter. Add the boiling water and stir gently, leveling out the cous cous so that it is all covered by the water. Once the water has been absorbed by the cous cous, carefully add the roasted vegetables to the pan and stir them in.

FENNEL & RADISH SALAD

Ingredients:

A bunch of water cress (chopped)
A Bulb of fennel (sliced very thinly)
8 radish (thinly sliced)
100g Feta cheese (cubed)
Olive oil
Salt & black pepper
Juice of half a lime
Salt & ground black pepper

Combine the ingredients in a salad bowl and drizzle with oil and lime juice, season to taste with salt & pepper.

67

Leaving Taghazout was difficult. I'd only been there a few days and already felt at home up at the park having met Ali and local young shredder Abdullah who was hilariously rude about my age and capacity on a board, "you dinosaur, why you skate?". It's easy to strike up a conversation in a skatepark, all you have to do is show up. The thought of tearing myself away from this incredible location and the prospect of a return to a British winter, was not met with much enthusiasm on my part. Back at my hotel, I took my time packing my bag, then sat drinking a soda in the market square as I waited for the taxi to take me to the airport. As I said my farewells, the thing that made leaving Taghazout a little easier was the thought of the next trip, a return to Palestine and a trip across the Allenby Bridge into Jordan. But as it turned out that was not to be. The global pandemic took hold just a couple of weeks after my return to England.

2020 turned out to be a year in which best laid plans were either abandoned, shelved or adapted. Little did I know it, but it turned out to be a number of weeks before I could get back on my board and feel the sense of creativity coursing through my veins.

Recipe:

1200 m2 of Land in Bull Bay, Jamaica
200 m3 of concrete
31 volunteers at the beginning
16 volunteers at the end
10 nationalities
1500 litres of Red Stripe beer
257 coconuts
8 hours of Reggae a day
2.5 kilograms of Jamaican Weed
6 puppies & 6 kittens born
2 songs composed
1 dick lighted on fire
1 curfew
1 state of emergency
1 fucking virus
24 flights cancelled
Limitless amounts of love & fun!

(Arthur Bonal in Across Tides zine 2020)

LOCKDOWN

As happens from time to time with cooking, the recipe doesn't always turn out how you were expecting. I've always maintained that that doesn't really matter too much, as you can usually do something with whatever comes out of the oven or off the hob. Unless it's burned to a crisp, the chances are that whatever you have cooked will at least be edible. Make the most of what you've got and see if you can learn a lesson for next time.

The global pandemic of 2020 was almost my undoing, but I decided rather than to scrape the contents into the bin, I would make the most of what I have got. It would seem pretty churlish of me to shut up shop when so many of the Social Skate Projects across the world are currently making the most of what they have. From Jamaica to Jordan and beyond, volunteers are finding new ways to work under 'lockdown'. Just weeks into the pandemic *The Good Push Alliance*, an initiative set-up by *Skateistan* to support and share knowledge among skateboarding projects worldwide, began putting together an online resource pack for projects struggling under the new environment. Through a series of webinars and an online toolkit, volunteers and project coordinators found a way to communicate and share lessons and experiences.

With all of my travel plans cancelled and photo and research opportunities suddenly vanishing, it became obvious that I was going to have to find a different way of working too. I was moved by by a 'recipe' which featured in in Issue 1 of *Across Tides* zine. The Freedom Skatepark in Bull Bay, Jamaica was completed by Concrete Jungle Foundation (CJF) volunteers despite the pandemic. It's a recipe with a sense of victory, and one that you know is just going to work.

Part of the whole nature of skateboarding is about picking yourself up off the floor and getting back on your board. It's about learning to take the falls and using them to inform how you progress. As a late starter, I was initially embarrassed about taking a slam. I was worried about how others might see a bloke in his fifties eating concrete, afraid that I might look ridiculous, but I soon began to realise that slams are part of the whole package. There is no shame in taking a tumble, in fact part of learning to skate is about learning how to fall, to use the momentum and to roll out of a wipeout, or to drop to your knees and allow the pads to absorb the impact and slide out of trouble. It's about learning from your mistakes. In some ways, a skater's route out of a slam can be as steezy (stylish) as the trick they were trying to nail, maybe even more so.

There's a similar narrative which runs through learning to cook. We've all burned a slice of toast, but not everybody would think to break it up and use it as croutons in a bowl of caramelised onion soup (its a flavour match from heaven, try it!). Our failures in the kitchen can inform our culinary skills and improve the dishes that come afterwards. Learning to cook is an ordeal of trial and error. A recipe enables someone to repeat, or approximate the efforts of another. If a recipe is written well, then following it to the letter should result in a replica of the original, but it doesn't always work like that. Recipes are open to interpretation, the quality of ingredients can vary. By veering off recipe and including a little intuition, then that is where results begin to differ, and new variations of classic dishes can appear.

I'm in the process of learning back slashes on a mini ramp. There's a recipe for that. The wisdom goes, pump at the bottom, keep your eye on the coping, go weightless and you'll rarely hang up. But despite following the recipe, I only score once in every four or five tries. I can see that the more I do, the higher the success rate. It's a question of keep going, don't give up.

When the Covid hit, certainly in the beginning, it put an end to my endeavours at the skatepark. The back slashes went on hold for a while, but as the weeks of lockdown rolled on and on, I began a series of dawn raids on my local park. Knowing that I would have the place to myself at six o'clock in the morning, and that I wouldn't be putting myself, or anyone else, in danger, I was able to carry on with my learning, picking myself up again after each (admittedly and thankfully, fewer and further in between) slam.

With International travel off the agenda, it appeared I was going nowhere. But then, as so often happens in weird times, another opportunity presented itself. In all honesty though, I went looking for it myself. Way before lockdown I'd heard tell of a new skatepark being built just up the road from where I live. The rumours and the excitement rippled across the parks I was skating in and around Leeds. Scottish park building legend, Youngo and his Concreate crew had the contract to build a park in Horsforth. I tracked Youngo down on instagram and offered my services.

Back in the mid 1980s, I spent a sizeable part of my youth humping bricks and mortar around most of the building sites in Swindon. I was a hod carrier, and good at it. In my prime I could feed five bricklayers with muck and bricks all day long. It was a time when Swindon was becoming the fastest growing town in Europe and jobs were easy come by. I worked for an outfit called S&L Brick Co. Ray Scar & Pip Little were a couple brickies who soon cottoned-on to the subcontracting game and built up a crew of bricklayers fed by an athletic gang of labourers and hod carriers like me. I'd work for six months or so, save up enough money to go travelling, then come back and pick up my hod. That first week back on the sites after time off travelling was always a killer. Every muscle, joint and bone in my body would ache in a manner that suggested I'd been hit by a truck and then had it reverse over my broken body. The only way to get through it was to get up, stick the boots on and get back to work the next day. "Muck up!"

TAMING THE BEAST

I picked up a number of skills on the building sites, mainly by watching others. After a stint working for a guy called Oggie who taught me about laying shuttering and mixing concrete, I went on to fit designer kitchens for people with more money than sense. I fired off a message to @concreatingskateparks via instagram,

"Worked on sites as a hod carrier and then subbing off local council, repairing/replacing concrete paths, guttering, fencing etc. Had a spell fitting designer kitchens too. Been a while, but still got it! Have steel toes & hard hat. Give me a shout if you think you can use me!"

He got back to me a while later, "Hey Josh we might have a bit of work for you."

So it turns out that that first week back on the sites after a couple of months off travelling I mentioned, well it seems like a walk in the park. After the best part of twenty five years off site, the ache is much worse. I knew it was coming, and in a weird way I was looking forward to it, but what I didn't know was that it was going to take a whole lot longer than just a week to work my way through the pain barrier. It's a far cry from re-laying a concrete path to an old council house in rural Wiltshire. If only Oggie could see me now! He'd most likely have something to say about me not mixing it all by hand, but when its a 4m³ pour, I'm just thankful it comes in a truck and gets pumped into the transition. That's when the magic really begins.

THE PREP BEFORE THE POUR

Before the concrete arrives, there is the preparation, lots of preparation. Geometry was never my strong point at school. I can remember a few basic formulae, but angles and inclines were beyond my ken. I never thought that, while staring out the window, pretending to listen to what my old maths teacher Mr Scott was saying, would bare any relevance to a young punk rocker. He always suggested that it would come in handy one day. Suffice to say, he was right.

The best part of forty years later and i'm standing in the deep end of a ten foot kidney bowl, surrounded by radii. Though i'm not yet blessed with the skills to work them all out for myself yet, give me a piece of string, some 15mm ply and a jigsaw and I will cut you a 2.2m striker. The thing about working on a skater-built skatepark is that shapes and forms can change as the development takes place. It made me realise the skill and art that goes into building places like Taghazout, Asira Ash Shamalia and 7 Hills in Amman. Many of the social skate project builds across the world don't have the luxury of heavy plant and a concrete pump. Much of the grunt work is done by hand, often on a shoestring rather than a comprehensive budget with in-built contingency. The volunteers that give up their time, sweat, and on occasion blood, are total legends, each and every one of them. Respect.

Once the shuttering, strikers and steel rebar are fixed into place, a make-shift shelter is erected over the pour site to keep the wind and the sun off the concrete. Sun and wind will cause the concrete to set more rapidly, 'flashing' at different rates when exposed to the elements, when ideally you need the whole pour to behave in unison and set at an even(ish) rate. Then comes the concrete......

The recipe is a simple one; two parts sand, two parts cement and one part stone, with an option to up the quantity of stone if the sand is too soft. But with this recipe, it's not just about the quantities, it's about knowing exactly what to do with it once it arrives on site. Thankfully the mix is pumped directly into the shuttering, which has been meticulously wired with steel rebar, and expertly laid out a day or two before. Having said that, the act of putting the pipes for the concrete pump together and cleaning them all out afterwards is an ordeal in itself.

Once the concrete goes into the transition, usually pumped initially from the top and then poured in to the bottom of the slope, then you've got about two hours before the stuff starts to go off and becomes unworkable. Skilled hands spread out the mix, bringing it level to the top of the wooden 'strikers' which define the curve and give it shape. Next, the concrete is smoothed with a pole 'ressie', a large float on a long pole which allows you to reach the top of the transition. Even at this point, expert knowledge is required, knowing just when and how to manipulate the liquid rock. If the mix is a little wet, then there's time for a quick fag break giving it time to stiffen up a bit, but not too much.

From this point on, the second pass, the rest is done using hand 'ressies', smaller floats which are shaped to reflect the curve of the transition. The resin face of the float is rough and creates friction, drawing some of the moisture from the concrete and begins to smooth the surface. By now, the 'crete has settled into its form and stiffened enough to stay where it's meant to be. If its a tall slope, then a wooden platform is knocked into the face of the transition to enable the talent to continue with the hand ressieing and reach the top of the transition. Meanwhile others, like me, begin to 'pepper' the face, gently throwing small handfuls of 'crete into the low points. Even this part is a skill as you have to watch how the rest of the mix behaves as you toss grenades of wet 'crete at the face. Throw it too hard and there's the possibility of causing an avalanche, and believe, you don't want to do that.

Once the second pass is complete and an initial seal is spread over the surface of the concrete, the 'crete begins to behave itself (i'm not kidding, it's like a living creature with a mind of its own), out come the 'maggies'. The platform is removed and the subsequent holes filled in with, now rapidly stiffening 'crete. Maggies are floats with a magnesium face, again each shaped to reflect the curve of the transition. These are smoother than the 'ressies', creating less friction when passed over the setting face, but still drawing moisture from the depths of the pour. By now, the concrete will take the weight of a person on a 'surf board', a large piece of 3mm plywood to spread the load over a broad surface area. In the absence of the platform, the 'surf board' enables the maggie wizards to reach higher up the transition, while someone else leans over from the top and works their way down the slope. By now the 'peppering' becomes a much more delicate action, no longer lobbing grenades of 'crete at the face, but scattering much smaller amounts at any holes or low spots which come to light once the maggies begin their work.

It's worth mentioning at this point that the concrete is now well on its way to setting, not rock hard yet but increasingly difficult to shape any that's not already been formed. It's here that my old concrete skills come into play as I was tasked with keeping a good bit of the excess 'crete still alive by adding water and mixing by hand with a shovel. 'Porridge' is what the experts are after at this stage, with as few stones in as possible as they get harder to work down once the 'crete beneath really starts to go off.

With a smooth-looking surface and the finished shape in place, the frantic pace slows a little then out come the 'steelies' for the final couple of passes. Again, the steel floats produce even less friction and really begin the draw the last drops of moisture to the surface and with it the 'fat', a creamy form of the mix bereft of stone and perfect for filling any final holes. By the time the steelies have done their work, the surface of the transition is almost as smooth as glass, turning from dark to light grey as the moisture evaporates. At this point, all I have to do is begin to gather and clean the hand tools in a large bucket of water ready for the next pour.

One of the things that I missed once I quit working the building sites was the camaraderie among fellow labourers, the opportunity to grab a few moments for a fag and talk bollocks. We'd share a common bond in our efforts, each there for different reasons, be it a hungry family, or mortgage to feed, or a simple desire to earn money and travel the world, we were united in a greater task. It's at times like these that personalities emerge, quirks, traits and humour. The thing about working on a site full of skaters is that the commonality is enhanced by our love of the wooden toy. Youngo, Craig, Hem, Stu, Slim, James, Ian and Avid each bring with them their own skills, stories and points of view, and of course accents. Birmingham, Liverpool, Glasgow, Leeds and the Highlands, a melange of linguistic anomalies spouting nonsense and jokes. I imagine the scene on an international skate project build must be similar, but with cities spread further between, citizens striving together immersed in the common language which comes through building a skatepark.

Physical work demands energy. A labourer on a building site can burn in excess of 1,300 calories a day. That's about five bacon butties, or in Hem's case, just one skatepark sarnie!

Recipe - The Hemburger

2 slices of buttered sourdough bread

1 Fried egg

2 Rashers of bacon

4 thick slices of Manchego cheese

Half an avocado (sliced)

2 slices of fresh tomato

(Approximately 1,145 calories)

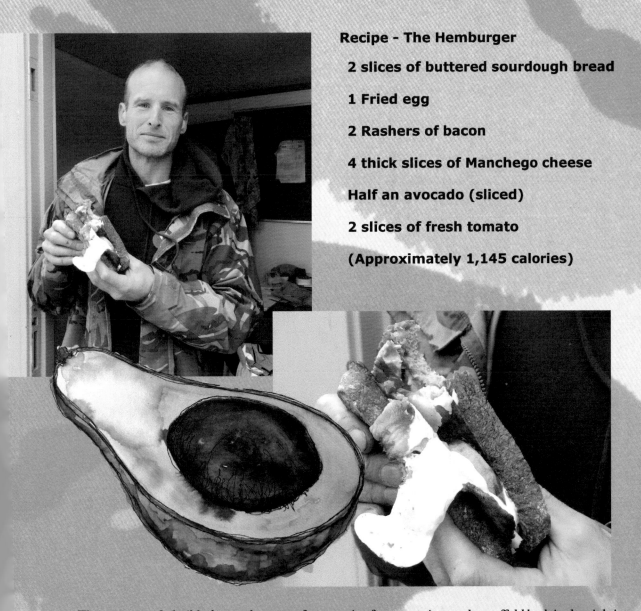

The contents of a builder's snap box was often a topic of conversation on the scaffold back in the eighties. Day in day out, the bricklayers I was supplying would moan about the sandwiches that their wives and partners had prepared for them, ham & egg, cheese & onion, spam. The same thing every day leads to culinary boredom, but always a topic of conversation. On the Horsforth build, The 'Hemburger' was a constant source of good humoured derission, but Hem always took the ridicule with a pinch of salt as it was intended.

I was saddened to hear that Hem sadly died in 2021. It truly was a pleasure working with and learning from him during my short time working on the Horsforth park. RIP Hem.

Recipe for a Skatepark

Ingredients:

Tons of concrete
Gallons of water
Miles of rebar
A wheelbarrow
A stack of volunteers
A couple of people who know what they're doing
A bunch of enthusiasm
Humour
Beer

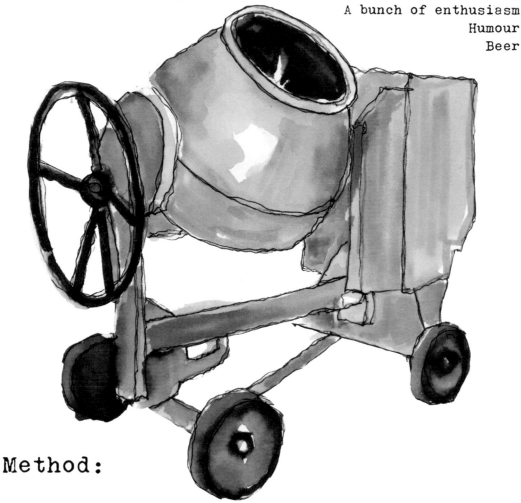

Method:

Dig, scrape, dig, dig, dig. Hump, shift, sweat. Rest, hump,
shift, sweat some more. Pause to sort out some paperwork
and a stroppy local government official. Dig some more, fit
rebar. Mix pour smooth. Skate the bit that's not finished
yet, mix and pour some more. Polish, polish, polish again.
Allow the concrete to bake in the sun for twelve hours. Have
a beer and a smoke, then skate the hell out of it.

I soon realised that there is a passion that goes in to building a skatepark that goes way beyond any financial consideration. The plethora of DIY skateparks worldwide, knocked together with crowdfunding and sheer determination bare testimony to that. During my time working with Concreate I rediscovered a vitality, and energy that comes through common endeavour. Although now in my mid fifties, I regained an enthusiasm for labour that somehow got lost in along the way through a series of office jobs and a career in food writing. Sure the physical graft is harder these days, for my ageing body, but once again the rewards, not to mention the new defined muscle tone, far outweigh any physical grumbles. The money comes in handy too, but it does trouble me that I helped build a pool that I'm, as yet, too scared to drop in to!

DON'T KNOW WHAT I WANT

BUT I KNOW HOW TO GET IT

DIY CULTURE AS ANARCHISM IN ACTION

The city is an irresistible magnet. For the young in small towns and villages where nothing ever happens, it pulls with the promise of variety and excitement. It draws those who chafe against the daily round and common task, those who feel that they can no longer stand Mum and Dad and the constraints they represent, those who know that back there in Deadsville there are going to be no jobs and no prospects, that nothing is ever going to happen. (Colin Ward: 1978)

As a kid growing up in a rural Yorkshire village during the 1970s and early 80s, I was desperate to get out. It wasn't so much 'deadsville' that drove me away, it was the promise of variety and excitement as I hitch-hiked my way to the next *New Model Army* gig and the adventures beyond. Through music, odd-jobbing as a roadie, merch vendor and general ligger, I stumbled through my twenties with no particular aim in life other than to explore the excitement that lay outside the tiny village where I grew up. And excitement there was aplenty. I travelled and lived abroad, learned languages, loved, laughed and lingered long in a world where I made it up as I went along. I was my own boss. But like so many others, and I'm not entirely sure how, I ended up with a proper job. A suit and a commute, and somehow, the lights went out. Thankfully, at more or less the same time, another light came on – family and children and all the joys that brings. It made the suit and commute bearable, and of course the money came in handy too. But before I knew it, a decade had gone by and despite the pleasures of family life (it's obviously not all a bed of roses) I missed that creative streak, the make it up as you go along, the do-it-yourself.

The community I've found through skateboarding is in many ways akin to visiting a new city for the first time, it's exciting. It is an irresistible magnet that draws me closer, attracting similar minds and never ceasing to amaze me in in its diversity. And at the heart of this community lies the notion of do-it-yourself. From zine-making, screen printing, painting and podcasting to film, photography and performance, skaters are enmeshed in a world of DIY. Iain Borden talks of an in-built, "ethos of self-reliance, inventive adaptation and unscripted adventure, which even stretches to the fabrication of ridable concrete." (Iain Borden: *Skateboarding and the city, 2019*).

Then redundancy hit me like a ton of bricks. But a pay-off and a foot up my arse was exactly what I needed to kick my creative mojo into action having lay dormant for way too long. I started writing, making it up again as I went along. My son introduced me to skateboarding at an age when most dads are looking to take things a bit easier. I will be forever indebted. For me, skateboarding has fuelled the creative DIY flame that re-erupted the day I burned my suit.

The first time I heard about DIY skateparks was in conversation with Yorkshire legend, skater and musician, *Serious Sam Barrett*. Sam talked about *New Bird*, *Needleside* and the *Dust Bowl* and a host of other DIY spots, the majority of which have fallen prey to the avarice of the urban developer, crushed in the jaws of Mammon. It became clear that not only do skaters adapt and learn to ride the physical environment around them, but they also *create* and shape the environments they operate in. DIY spots are often short-lived but have a lasting impact. The transferable skills that people bring to a build, as well as lessons learned in construction, enable them to find other like minds and build another. The way in which people come together and work together on a DIY build fascinates me.

It's nothing short of anarchy in action as described by architect and anarchist Colin Ward:

There are at least two kinds of organisation. There is the kind which is forced on you, the kind which is run from above, and there is the kind which is run from below, which can't force you to do anything, and which you are free to join or free to leave alone. We could say that the anarchists are people who want to transform all kinds of human organisation into the kind of purely voluntary association where people can pull out and start one of their own if they don't like it.

(Ward: 1966 - Anarchism as a theory of organisation)

Whilst DIY builders may not necessarily wish to transform all kinds of human organisation into voluntary association, the way in which they organise themselves – *voluntary, functional, temporary* and *small* in number sits well with Ward's anarchist theory of organisation. Voluntary, preserving individual freedom to come and go and participate or not, as one pleases. The small, functional and temporary nature of a DIY build crew ensures that hierarchies and organisational bodies don't have time to set-in, focus is on the work that needs doing rather than determining and defining the structure of the group. There is no bureaucracy. A range of skills and experience are brought together and compliment the group, no one person is 'in charge'.

With the recent growth in popularity of skateboarding, to some extent fuelled by its proposed inclusion as an olympic sport, the number of 'official' (municipally sanctioned) skateparks is on the increase. There are currently upward of twenty five skatepark construction companies in the UK alone, but DIY spots continue to erupt, anarchistic in their defiance of authority and spreading like a rash across the face of capitalist endeavour.

"Anarchy" clearly has market appeal, it helped launch the Sex Pistols onto an international stage, it lends its name to a skate brand. The classic 'A' in a circle emblem can be found splashed across T-Shirts, pin badges and merchandise the world over, but such ventures appear to have little to do with a specific political ideology and more to do with earning 'cash from chaos'. DIY skatepark building on the other hand is entirely the opposite, it *costs* money to build and maintain a DIY, there is little to be made out of it.

In a society where land comes at a premium and is largely earmarked for development by speculative entrepreneurs, cash-strapped local authorities will often bow to the power of the developer in the hope of catching a few crumbs by way of a Unilateral Undertaking or a Section 106 Agreement obliging the developer to 'give something back' to the city. Many DIY spots exist in this 'hinterland', on waste ground or pockets of land, suspended in time, awaiting a decision from the local planning authority. The arrival of skaters with barrow-loads of a can-do attitude, sand, cement, shovels, ressies, a couple of cases of beer, and a bag of weed, breathes necessary life, into these otherwise empty spaces. City planners and architects have long since recognised the need to create space for play in high density urban areas, hemmed-in by fast moving traffic. Ward, again, suggests that;

The authoritarian response to this need is to provide an area of tarmac and some pieces of expensive ironmongery in the form of swings, see-saws and roundabouts which provide a certain amount of fun (though because of their inflexibility children soon tire of them) but which call for no imaginative or constructive effort on the child's part, and cannot be incorporated in any self chosen or reciprocal activity. Swings and roundabouts can only be used in one way, they cater for no fantasies, for no developing skills (Ward: 1996 - Anarchy in action)

The hundreds of steel & composite ramps rusting and rotting unused in distant corners of playing fields up and down the country stand as testament to this. A 'this'll do' attitude taken by many local councils in authoritarian ignorance, often with little or no consultation offered to end users.

I'm loathe to refer to skaters as 'children', though many are of course, but the construction of a DIY spot strikes me as viable response to the problem of a 'lack of imaginative or constructive effort', indeed DIY construction through its very nature requires imagination and a deal of constructive effort. And as for skills, not only are skills learned in the construction of a DIY, but they are also honed in the riding of the thing once complete.

Far from the 'chaotic', 'destructive' or even 'violent' misconception held by many, anarchism, as Ward reminds us, "in all its guises is an assertion of human dignity and responsibility. It is not a programme for political change but an act of social self-determination." (Ward: 1996 - Anarchy in action). Anarchism is not tied to any one particular manifesto, it breeds freedom of thought and freedom to act without authority.

As long as viable pockets of land continue to lie unused, weed, needle, and shopping trolley-strewn, while their owners languish ankle-deep in red tape shelling-out backhanders in the local planning department, DIY culture and construction will continue to flourish as anarchism in direct action. It is a key element of skateboard culture, celebrated in *Love Letters* and *Confusion*, and increasingly shaping the future of British skateboarding, while slowly gaining recognition among some forward-thinking city planners.

I recently visited The Grove DIY in London. Situated just off the South Circular in Dulwich, the park sprang up in the carpark of the Grove public house after a group of local volunteers spotted the skatepark

potential back in early 2020. Some three years later the Grove has grown to include a community garden, growing fresh produce for skaters and members of the community to use. Similarly, Bournbrook DiY in Selly Oak, Birmingham sprang up on a recreational green space that had been left in decline for many years and in effect become a no-go zone for members of the public. Through the endeavours of volunteer skaters and their fund-raising capacity, Bournbrook has become the first DIY park in the UK to gain official skatepark status in the eyes of a local authority.

Another park, Hackney Bumps in north London has recently been transformed by volunteers and members of the local community pursuing the DIY ethic. Originally built back in 1986 as a cycle park, Hackney Bumps consisted of series of gently undulating humps and moguls designed for the entertainment of two-wheeled riders in the heyday of BMX riding. Henry Kingsford offers an eye-popping history in *Grey* skate mag:

"The Bumps were built ... just before Thatcher's government decision to disband the Greater London Council was implemented. The park cost £250,000, which would be expensive by today's standards but 34 years ago was astronomical."

Grey, vol 05, issue 06 (2020)

Clearly built in the rush to spend before the money ran out, the Bumps sadly fell victim to a lack of funding once the GLC had finally gone. The park fell into disrepair and became a dumping ground for burned-out stolen motorcycles, used needles, mangled BMX bikes and the ubiquitous abandoned shopping trolly. Having deteriorated in the intervening years, the notoriously rough surface of the park deterred most skateboarders, with the exception of a couple of local skaters. Henry Kingsford takes up the story again in his piece for *Grey*:

The Hackney Bumps regeneration project came about when two local skaters - Greg King and Nick Tombs ... found themselves skating and hanging out at the Bumps out of convenience, but : "not really having the best time," as Greg explained ... "We'd be like: 'somebody should really do something about this place,' and then one day we were like: 'Oh I guess it's going to be us then.'

Grey, vol 05, issue 06 (2020)

By September 2019, Nick and Greg's skateboarding DIY ethos lead to the formation of a community trust which found itself in negotiations with Hackney Borough Council and a branch of Sport England, in a bid to restore the park beyond its former glory. Then shortly after, just as encouraging noises were being made by potential funders, everything came to a standstill as Covid 19 spread its ugly wings over the planet. With new trust members, Esther Sayers and Daryl Knobbs on board, the project found a way to keep moving forward. Daryl brought with him several years of expertise having worked in the skatepark construction business in Norway and in England prior to that. Daryl who introduced the idea of grinding the surface of the heavily decayed concrete back to a smooth finish, a technique he had picked up while working with Betongpark across Scandinavia. With a polishing machine and a grinding pad, he set about testing a small area of the park. It worked!

With financial negotiations at a standstill, and while Greg and Nick were furloughed, the team set about polishing the whole of the park by themselves from their own pocket. It wasn't long before the local community showed up to help out and a crowd-funder was established to help cover the cost of the grinding pads. By the time I visited back August 2020, shortly after the addition of a few ledges, hips and quarters built under Daryl's watchful eye. Cleared of the junk and debris that once rendered this community space another no-go zone, Hackney Bumps had become a fully-fledged skatepark, once again in use by the whole community. With the help of locals, Esther, Nick, Greg and Daryl had managed to rejuvenate what had become a hot spot hangout for drug users and 'undesirables' and turn it into a safe family space where people could learn to skate, ride bikes and scooters and socialise together. It bore an uncanny similarity to the Love Park in Philadelphia, where once the skaters moved in, the place became a safe haven for other users. This seems to be a familiar pattern where skaters are concerned. City planners take note.

A mere five or ten minutes roll away from the Bumps you'll find Ridley Road market. A wander around here is like taking a stroll around the equator, a meander between the tropics of Capricorn and Cancer. An amazing, mesmerizing array of fruit, vegetables and fish (dried and fresh) greet the eyes and shopping bags of all who go there. If the original idea of this book was to present recipes inspired by the different countries in which skate projects have taken root, then a visit to Hackney presents a bit of a puzzle. In this chapter you will find a compendium of recipes drawn, not from one region or country, but from one street in London. It's a jam, a melting pot of culture and cuisine clinging by the skin of its teeth to a space threatened by the solid creep of gentrification.

RIDLEY ROAD E8
LONDON BOROUGH OF HACKNEY (BUMPS)

My first experiences of Ridley Road date back to the mid eighties and late night/early morning acid-fuelled trips to the 24 hour bagel shop, where other creatures of the night could sate their munchies on cream cheese and salmon. It was an exciting time as a nineteen year old discovering new worlds, both real and cerebral, and a far cry from the rural Yorkshire village where I'd grown up. Apart from anything the very concept of any shop being open for twenty four hours, let alone a paradise of palette pleasers where chemically-induced hunger pangs could be sated with protein and carbohydrate, was a marvel difficult to fathom for a young lad in a lysergic state of mind.

Sadly, the bagel shop was no longer there on my recent trip (it might not even have been there on my previous trips, but mutual recollections among friends assure me otherwise) and to be honest the market was looking a little forlorn, almost past its sell by date.

Like Hackney Bumps before its refurb, Ridley Road market has suffered the ravages of time. Established a century before the Bumps, from its outset in the 1880s the market has been a place where visitors could buy fruit, vegetables and other foodstuff from far flung corners of the earth. But recent years and the scars of capitalist greed and the cancerous creep of gentrification have threatened the market, as well as the surrounding area. Ridley Road market was, is and has been known for its affordability, ensuring that the prospect of a decent meal is within reach of the vast majority of household budgets.

SMOKEY PULLED JACKFRUIT

Ingredients:

A glug of olive oil
A knob of butter
A large onion (chopped)
2 cloves of garlic (chopped)
3 or 4 sun-dried tomatoes (chopped finely)
Salt & black pepper
100g chestnut mushrooms (chopped)
1 tsp paprika
1 tsp smoked paprika
1 tin of chopped tomatoes
1 tbsp tomato puree
A dash of dark soy sauce
A dash of Henderson's Yorkshire Relish
(You can use Worcester sauce as an alternative)
1 tin of jackfruit pieces (400g)

Heat the olive oil and butter in a deep sided frying pan, add the onion and cook for a good ten minutes. Once the onion begins to caramelise, throw in the chopped garlic and finely chopped sun-dried tomatoes. Cook for a minute or so and add the chopped mushrooms along with the seasoning and both types of paprika. Stir well then add the tin of tomatoes and the tomato puree together with the rest of the ingredients, stir again and place a lid on the pan and turn the heat down low. Allow to simmer very gently for twenty five minutes until the jackfruit begins to soften. Remove the lid and using a pair of forks, carefully shred the pieces of jackfruit to break them up.

Serve in a warm buttered baguette with a side of coleslaw if you like.

ROAST BUTTERNUT SQUASH & FETA SALAD

INGREDIENTS:

1 Butternut Squash
1 Red onion (peeled, halved lengthways and cut into slices)
A handful of pine kernels
200g Feta Cheese
A bunch of flat leaf parsley (chopped)
1 tbsp black mustard seed
1 tsp Sumac
Olive oil
Juice of half a lime

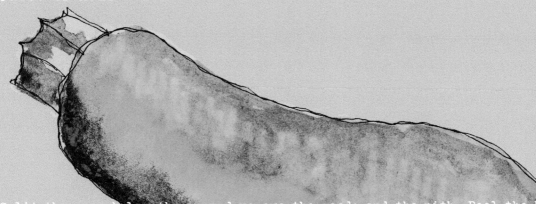

Split the squash lengthways and remove the seeds and the pith. Peel the hard outer-skin and cut the squash into 2cm cubes. Place on a baking tray along with the onion and the pine kernels. Drizzle with olive oil and roast in the oven at 200c for twenty five minutes. Remove from the oven and allow to cool completely.

Cut the Feta into 1cm cubes and place in a salad bowl along with the roasted squash, onion and pine kernels. Drizzle with good quality olive oil and the lime juice, then throw in the sumac, the mustard seeds and the chopped flat leaf parsley. Use your fingers or a pair of salad servers to mix it all through.

Ingredients:

500g waxy potatoes
A sprig of fresh rosemary
125g haloumi
1 tsp smoked sweet paprika
1 egg (beaten)
Ground black pepper
A pinch of dried chili flakes
Oil for frying

ROSTI

Par-boil the potatoes whole for six or seven minutes. Remove from the pan and allow to cool. Strip the leaves from the rosemary and chop very finely. Once cooled enough to handle, grate the potatoes into a large mixing bowl and throw in the chopped rosemary. Grate the haloumi into the bowl and add the paprika, pepper and chili flakes. Pour in the beaten egg and stir through with a wooden spoon to make sure the ingredients are evenly distributed throughout.

Warm a little oil in a non-stick frying pan and add the grated rosti mix. Spread evenly over the pan with the back of the wooden spoon and cook over a moderate heat for five minutes. Turn out the rosti onto a lightly oiled plate (see diagram opposite), return to the pan to cook the other side for a further five minutes or until the rosti is a lovely golden brown.

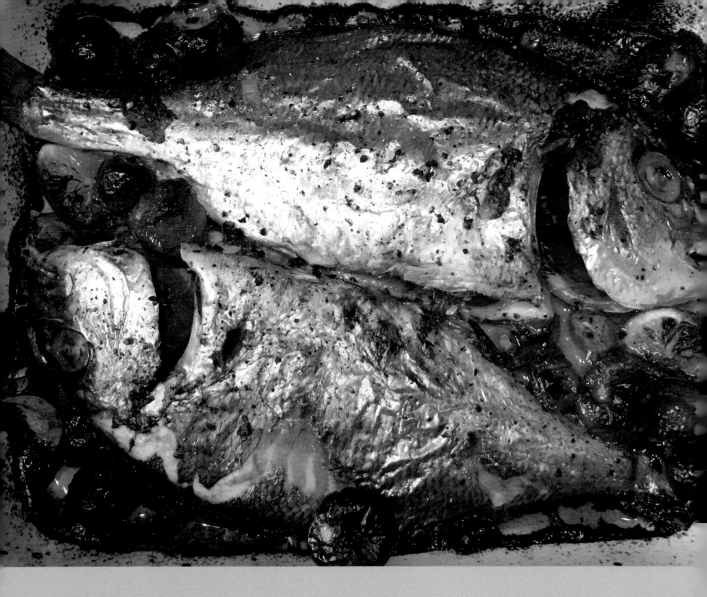

2 fresh sea bream (cleaned and gutted)
2 large sprigs of fresh thyme
A couple of knobs of butter
1 tbsp fennel seed
1 tsp whole black peppercorns
A handful of cherry tomatoes
6 cloves of garlic (skin left on)
1 lime (cut into wedges)
Salt & ground black pepper
A splash of white wine
Olive oil

Pre-heat the oven to 180° centigrade. Place a sprig of thyme, a wedge of lime and a knob of butter inside each fish. Pop them in a baking dish. Scatter the fennel seed and peppercorns over the fish and arrange the cherry tomatoes and cloves of garlic around the outside. Squeeze the juice from the remaining lime wedges over the fish and throw them in too. Pour in a splash of white wine and drizzle with a generous amount of olive oil and season with salt & pepper. Bake in the oven for 25-30 minutes.

BAKED ANGRY LOOKING
SEA BREAM

SATURDAY NIGHT.
BANGOR PIER
????

Airport — £40
Food Penzance — £18
Food Cambridge — £25.
LONDON LEZ — £17.50
Re Diesel Camb — £140.
Pool
£240 ÷ 4

fuel stop
£80 (Nett)

FULL PIPE
Too Much Water

28812
27496

1,316 miles

Total fuel.
= £460.
66 litres.

Diesel @ £10 Gallon

Roughly 23 mpg.
19 mpG

ROAD TRIP

BEATS WORKIN'

GRUND SUPPLY

AIR CULTURE

FREESTILE

THE STAR INN

SUNDAY NIGHT ????

WAVE GRAVEL

FUEL STOP
MAGNUS £80

FUEL STOP (Near) £80

?

HELDOVER HOLIDAYS CAMPSITE
TR7

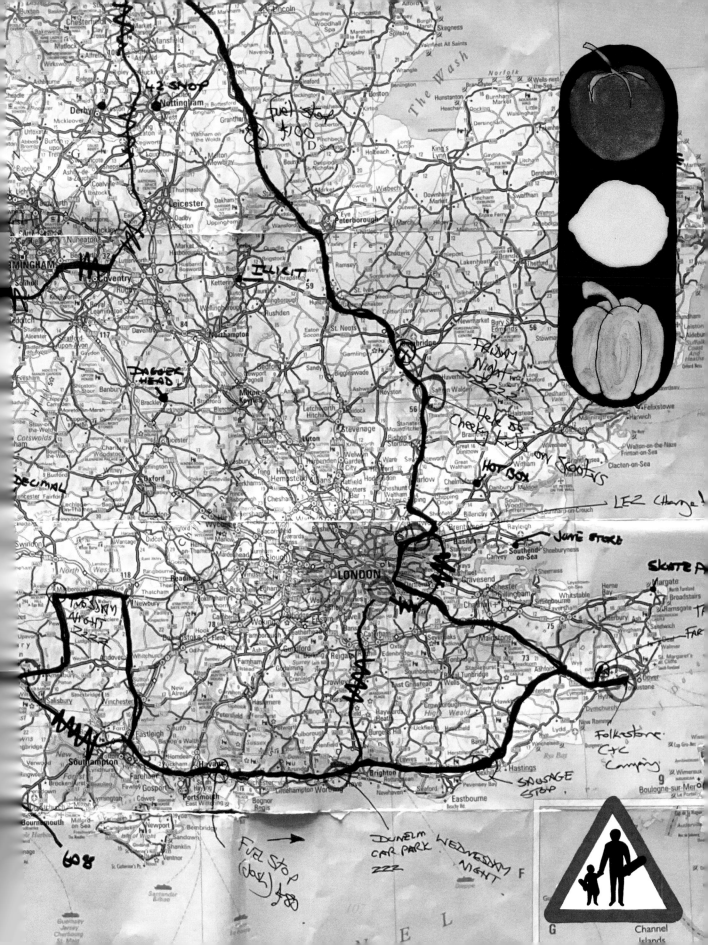

NOW YOU'RE EITHER ON THE BUS, OR YOU'RE OFF THE BUS

An Englishman, A Swede, A frenchman and an American climb into a luxury motorhome... It sounds like the beginning of a dodgy joke. No joke but plenty of laughs.

With a combined age of two hundred and twenty eight years, the four of us set off on a week-long tour of UK skateparks, covering some 1,400 miles and devouring approximately 46 gallons of diesel and several beers en-route. At the time of booking the motorhome, I was a little reluctant to tell the owners at Thistle Motorhome Hire in Knaresborough what we were up to, as skateboarders tend to have a reputation as hell raisers. But when I went to collect the van I confessed and Dougie the owner seemed genuinely interested in the idea and not in the least bit phased. So with our hell raising days several decades behind us, we set off along the M62 bound for Bangor and a lovely time was had.

The idea for the skate trip came from an afternoon spent skateboarding in October 2021, with a French friend of a friend in Fuveau just outside Marseille. In fact, it's probably worth while at this point mentioning just how I ended up with this 'friend of a friend'. Back in 2019 I was on my way to a Guild of Food Writers committee meeting in London. I'd got to Leeds train station and was enjoying a coffee and a bacon buttie in Pret, when suddenly my back went - for no particular reason, it just went. I was incapacitated. With plenty of time before my train departed, I lay down on the floor outside Pret and waited for the twinge to pass. It didn't. As departure time crept closer, I managed to hobble as far as the ticket barrier, using my skateboard as a rather too short crutch. Once through the barrier, I sat down on a bench in absolute agony. It didn't look like I was going to make the train. Here's where things began to improve (not the pain mind, just things). A member of the station staff spotted me wincing on the bench as came over to enquire as to my well-being. I explained what had happened and he immediately offered to bring me a cup of tea from the office. With tea in hand I watched as the 09:15 to London King's Cross pulled out of Leeds station. I phoned in my apologies to the committee. Still unable to move, and thankful for the tea, I remained on the bench for another hour or so, when I was approached by another kind stranger asking as to my well-being. Christophe, had spotted my skateboard and could see that I was in some sort of difficulty, being a skateboarder himself, he sat down and chatted with me for half an hour or so while waiting for his train. I learned that he was from Marseille and now living and working in North Yorkshire. He told me of a pool, a concrete skate pool built by an enthusiast in the countryside somewhere near Aix-en Province, the Holenite pool. It sounded scary. Christophe went on his way, but we kept in touch via social media. I ended up being pushed in a wheelchair across the station, where I managed to crawl into a taxi which took me to A&E at Leeds General Infirmary, again using my skateboard as a crutch I made my way, very slowly, into the waiting area and after a little waiting, was plied with painkillers and sent on my way.

So a couple of years later, and ahead of a short family holiday to Marseille, I contacted Christophe for a few tips on the best spots to skate in Marseille. "Just hook-up with my pal Jean" he said and gave me Jean's contact details. Jean told me to hop on a bus to Aix-en-Province and he'd pick me up there. He took me to his local pool in Fuveau and we had a blast. Skateboarding is like that, you can show up anywhere in a foreign town with your skateboard and find someone to skate with, in this case I already had a lead, a connection. It's one of the many things that I discovered as I got further into my own skateboarding journey, there is a camaraderie among skaters, regardless of ability, but founded on the stoke.

My companions on this trip were veteran skaters, and had all been skateboarding on and off since the 1980s. I hoping to learn a thing or two on the way.

Jean, 57 and a secondary school history teacher in Aix-en-Provence, contacted me some weeks after I had returned from that family holiday to Marseille saying he had an idea. While visiting him at his home in Fuveau, I'd been flicking through a book called 'Poolaroids' by Mark 'Trawler' Lawler. The book is a fairly comprehensive collection of photographs and reviews of skateparks across the UK. It caught my eye not least because of the stunning photography, but also because Horsforth, the skatepark I'd helped build was in there. Jean suggested a tour of UK skateparks might be an interesting adventure. He added a caveat; they must have a pool. A 'pool' is just that, like a backyard swimming pool, but built purposely for skating with concrete coping and tiles around the lip which make a satisfying noise as your wheels roll over them. Pools can be difficult to skate, so I knew that it wasn't all going to be plain sailing.

Jean emailed me a list of the parks from Trawler's book that he said he'd like to visit. I like a challenge, "leave it with me" I said. I contacted a pal, Jono who happens to be one of the most radical pool riders in the country (he'd never admit to that himself) and a good pal I skate with regularly at Horsforth. Jono immediately whittled the list down to a more manageable number and I pretty quickly devised an itinerary which meant that we could probably visit all ten in just one week. Within less than a dozen emails and about three or four weeks, Jean had put a crew together.

We were joined on the trip by Magnus, a history teacher from Stockholm and the oldest in our troop at 58 and Jeff from LA. Jeff was the youngest, at a mere 51 years of age. Jeff runs the largest skatepark directory website in the world, *Concrete Disciples*, and has skated with some of the great names; Tony Hawk, Rodney Mullen to name just two. To be honest, all three of my new-found companions have skated with big names in skateboarding. The names of famous and professional skaters from around the world were bouncing round the cabin of the motorhome for the whole trip. Most of whom, I'd never even heard of, but what do I know?

What did strike me was Jean's capacity to recall the names of skaters from the 70s and 80s as well as their particular styles and tricks. He seemed to know about everyone. I just kept my eyes on the road

The bus handled like a dream. It had been a while since I was at the wheel of such a large vehicle, but by the time I'd navigated my way out of Knaresborough, I'd pretty much got the hang of it. Dougie the owner had given me the comprehensive lowdown on operating the essentials, heating, fridge, cooker and of course the on-board loo, so I set sail for the airport to gather the last of the crew. Jean was the last aboard and just about five minutes after I'd engaged cruise control on the M62, Jeff got a message on his socials inviting us all along to the YoYo Pool, a private backyard pool somewhere near Wigan. What a start! I'd never ridden a backyard pool, and this one was legendary not least because it's home to 'YoYo's Pool Cats', a girl skate crew hailing from Wigan. Dave, the owner and builder of the pool had been following Jeff's adventures since he'd arrived in the UK and had gathered that we were heading west out of Leeds, 'drop in, its on the way'.

With music blaring and beers flowing (not me guv, I'm driving!) copings were ground and front rocks sent. There might have been a couple of stalefish, fastplants and laybacks going on but in all honesty I haven't got a clue what tricks are what. The moves that make up a trick happen so fast to my eye that I can't even discern what's happening. It's kind of like trying to judge a high diving competition, there are so many twists and turns that I just can't make out what's happening, was that a double pike or a triple? I just knew that thanks to the locals who'd shown up for the session and Dave's impeccable hospitality, I was having the time of my life and we hadn't even reached the first scheduled pool yet. There's a spontaneity to skateboarding that appears inherent to its practice, 'yeh I'll give that a go, see what happens'. It's the only way to make progress. The buzz around that pool was a two way thing, Dave and the others were equally stoked to have us, as we were to be there.

We reached Bangor in the dead of night and pulled up in the car park next to the pier. I'd been there a couple of years before and remembered it as a dead cert place to stop over. All the level ground spots were taken, so out came the yellow levelling chocks and a few 'back a bit' and 'forward to the left a bit' commands from Jeff resulted in a reasonably level park up.

Heading south from Bangor later that morning, we set off for Hereford, but got waylaid by a search for a full pipe that Jeff had come across via his socials. Somewhere near Telford there is a flood defence system with a huge concrete pipe running under the A5. Opting to check it out meant missing Hereford, but like I said, there's a spontaneity to skateboarding.

We took in Newport, Newquay and St Ives. Thankfully Newquay and St Ives proved entirely skateable for this ageing beginner and whilst I was nowhere near the skill level of my contemporaries, much fun was had and no bones broken. The journey east to Shoreham on day four was broken with a non skating day heading, via Stonehenge, to an overnight stay in the beautiful Savernake Forest just outside Marlborough in Wiltshire. A night spent on a Camping and Caravanning Club site in the middle of an ancient forest made a pleasant change from roadside lay-bys and harbour car parks.

Heading south from Bangor later that morning, we set off for Hereford, but got waylaid by a search for a full pipe that Jeff had come across via his socials. Apparently he had seen Sean Goff and a pal riding it up on You Tube. Somewhere near Telford there is a flood defence system with a huge concrete pipe running under the A5. Despite it being the hottest, driest summer for decades, there was too much water running through it to skate. Opting to check it out of course meant missing Hereford, but like I said, there's a spontaneity to skateboarding.

We took in Newport, Newquay and St Ives. Thankfully Newquay and St Ives proved entirely skateable for this ageing beginner and whilst I was nowhere near the skill level of my contemporaries, much fun was had and no bones broken. The journey east to Shoreham on day four was broken with a non skating day heading, via Stonehenge, to an overnight stay in the beautiful Savernake Forest just outside Marlborough in Wiltshire. A night spent on a Camping and Caravanning Club site in the middle of an ancient forest made a pleasant change from roadside lay-bys and harbour car parks.

Shoreham proved a challenge. It took me about twenty minutes to pluck up the courage to drop in to the clover shaped pool, but it was worth it. The split second feeling of weightlessness at the drop-in gives way to a feeling of elation as you realise that you're still standing on your board and now rolling at speed over smooth concrete and heading for the lip at the other side of the pool. Cheers of encouragement from my fellow travellers and the old guy regulars who'd showed up for a session, rang out around the park, drowning out the sound of The Clash blaring from the boombox. An evening swim in the Channel and a couple of pints in the Duke of Wellington pub with the Shoreham locals after the session capped-off my favourite day of the trip so far.

High on my list was the brand new multi-million pound multi-storey purpose-built skatepark, F51 in Folkestone. I've been following its development with enthusiasm on Instagram for the past couple of years, but would have to wait until day six of the trip to explore this wonder of the skateboarding world. The project was funded, in part at least, by the Roger De Haan Charitable Trust, a fact that gave rise to much laughter as I explained to my middle-aged companions that we were on a pilgrimage to a skatepark funded by the one time owner of the Saga group of companies. It seemed fitting.

Navigating an eight-metre motorhome around Folkestone's one way system is not the easiest task, especially when the vehicle is full of ageing skaters, eager to get parked up and ride the country's first ever purpose-built multi-storey skatepark. Jeff's persuasive powers and Californian charm came in handy in securing a parking spot right outside the building, having made at least three runs around the one way system in an effort to find the entrance to the car park. Funded by the Roger De Haan charitable trust, and run by sports charity The Sports Trust, F51 opened in April 2022. With a concrete bowl room on the first floor and two wooden floors, a street section above and a 'flow' room on the top floor, we'd found our Mecca. The place even has showers, a much needed luxury after a full-on two-hour skateboarding session.

Back in the van and finally heading north after a week on the road the four of us were in agreement that the adventure had been a blinding success. We took in Rom skatepark on the outskirts of London and the pool at Saffron Walden on the trip back north. Rom is one of the oldest parks in the country, built in 1978 and now has Grade II listed status. It was way too gnarly for Magnus and I to ride, but Jeff and Jean ripped it to pieces.

Saffron Walden was a blast, until the local scooter kids showed up and chased us off their patch. Running away from a group of cocky teenagers was perhaps not our finest moment, but there's only so much lip an old guy can take. We landed back in Leeds after a full week on the road, no broken bones or bruised egos (what goes on in Saffron Walden stays in Saffron Walden) and not a single argument! The only dilemma was where we are heading next, the south of France, Sweden or California?

CRUSHING MODELOS AND STACKING CLIPS

Government of the rich by the rich for the rich

When I told my now 16 year old son that I was heading off to University of San Diego to a conference on skateboarding, he looked up from his GCSE (General Certificate of Stress Endurance!) revision and asked, "Is that a thing? You mean I could go to university and study skateboarding?" "Yes son, keep revising", I said. To be perfectly honest I was thinking of doing a Hunter S Thompson and blowing the gig once I got there. The legend of Thomson missing the 'Rumble in the Jungle' (the Foreman - Ali fight held in Kinshasa in 1974), in favour of floating around in a swimming pool and smoking weed, appealed to my inner, long-since dormant, drug fiend. I figured I'd find a pool or two of my own to play in once I touched down in San Diego, but the reality of the matter is that I'm less keen on the drugs these days. Besides, skipping a gig like this would be just plain dumb. I'd arranged the trip a number of weeks previously, hooking up with a couple of skateboarding academics I'd 'met' via social media but never 'IRL' after I'd bagged my flight. With a bed in an Air B'n'B booked in Ocean Beach, sharing with eight of the said academics, I set off on the long journey to the Californian coast.

Thanks to an overnight in London and the most excellent hospitality of an old pal, I had chance to take-in the 'Beyond the Streets' exhibition at the Saatchi Gallery in Sloane Square. The first time I'd visited the Saatchi was at a private viewing arranged by my Art Foundation course tutor Grant Devine, back in the 80s, when the gallery was up in St John's Wood. The handful of mushrooms that I'd dropped as we arrived in London added an extra (unseen by my fellow art students) layer of WOW to the Warhol exhibition, such that by the time the curator got round to asking if we seventeen-year-olds had any poignant questions, the only query I could muster was, "where are the toilets?" as the psilocybin was firing urgent messages to my bladder. But like I say, I'm less keen on the drugs these days. The twenty five quid entry for to the Beyond the Streets exhibition was extortionate, but to be fair they had filled four floors of this enormous building with photographs, prints, a host of ephemera, and other paraphernalia evoking 'street culture' going back some decades. I was kind of stoked when I got to the Beastie Boys/Run DMC display and seeing photos, tickets and backstage passes from the gig in 1987 at Brixton Academy, to which I went alone and had my mind blown. The exhibition was in its way, the most suitable launch-pad for my sojourn, Hip-Hop, graffiti, skateboarding and a bunch of old punk posters from the Mott Collection presented the perfect portal to *The Stoke Sessions: An International Conference on the Culture, History and Politics of Surfing and Skateboarding.*

BRITISH AIRWAYS
SUTTON/JOSHUA MR
BA 272 24APR
SAN DIEGO LONDON
SEAT 53C
GATE 51 BOARD AT 1820 GATE CLOSE GROUP 4
BA/BLUE0049571E WORLD TRAVELLER BAGS 1/19

HAVE YOU SEEN HIM?

ACADEMY THEATRE
THURSDAY MAY 28
STALLS
Run DMC
AND THE BEASTIE BOYS
Nº 118

TRINITY HALL
COMMUNITY CENTRE
ASHTON COURT
FESTIVAL BENEFIT
CRASS
AND THE
Poison Girls
WEDS 18 JUNE
8PM £1.00

118

Several hours, four or five films, three double whiskies and approximately six small bottles of wine later, we touched down with a bump in San Diego. Hooking up with Tom, Ben and Liz who had also just stepped off the flight from Heathrow, we Ubered our way to our air b 'n' bungalow in Ocean Beach packed with three professors and five phd students. I'm still not sure if it was because I was the oldest in the house, but I was allowed first choice of bed so I opted for a bottom bunk preferring to sleep alone rather than share a king-size bed with a stranger possibly given to citing academic theorem in their sleep. Despite all of my housemates giving presentations up at the university every day during the three day conference, we found time to skate the nearby Robb Field skatepark, which apparently happens to be Neil Blender's local park. There he was pushing around on his weird little inverted Heated Wheel board with the narrowest of trucks. There was too much flat bottom and coastal eroded concrete for my liking, but it was fun and I did learn to 50-50 grind the mini baby pools outside the park, so that was definitely a win.

Three days of academic conference, sinking Modelo beers and Hot BBQ beef sandwiches from Chris' Liquor store and delicatessen were accented with skate sessions at Washington Street (terrifying!), Linda Vista (amazing) and the Chicano DiY underneath a freeway. I was stoked when Jeff, my travelling companion on the pool tour in the previous chapter, got in touch and travelled down from Los Angeles for the day on the Saturday. It was thanks to him and his rental car that I got to visit Washington Street and Linda Vista skate parks.

Up at SDSU the conference was in full swing, following an opening evening with the Hawk brothers, Tony and Steve, in conversation. The banality of the conversation was broken by Tony's comment describing his first encounter with Kelly Slater's wave generating machine as a kind of 9/11 moment. I was unsure as to whether Tony was referring to the invention of the wave machine as a catastrophic disaster, or a merely a 'world-changing' moment, either way the conversation was wrapped up shortly after that and the fans were left to pose for selfies with the local boy legend of skateboarding.

Talks and presentations ran all day across a number of lecture halls and rooms. The simultaneous presentations meant that I had to choose carefully which sessions I wanted to attend. Keen to dust off my own academic acumen and tease my brain, I joined sessions muting the idea of "skatepark re-use of colonialized brownfield land as a case of decolonialization" (Dr Brian Glenney) and "Grey Spaces: Skateboarding in the Anthropocene" (Dr Paul O'Connor). In all honesty I struggled to fully grasp the concepts being discussed. Dr Glenney's presentation seemed to suggest that those skateparks built on brownfield sites, land that had been 'colonised' by industry and often left polluted once that industry had closed or move elsewhere, could be seen as 'decolonising' that land by bringing it back into public use. A concrete skatepark performs the role of 'capping-off' polluted land, containing contaminants beneath. This idea seemed to me to dis-prove the old adage that 'you can't polish a turd', and whilst completely lacking in any form of academic nuance, I suggested as such at the end of the presentation to no little amusement of the audience. Having completely revealed my lack of understanding of the philosophical issues being discussed, I decided to keep my mouth shut for the duration of Dr O'Connor's discussion on 'Grey Spaces', though a gag on my lack of grey matter did cross my mind. I thoroughly enjoyed Tom Critchley's presentation on the Grove DiY project in south London where a group of skaters have built a skatepark in the grounds of a long-closed old London pub. Referencing the cultural significance of its location just off the South Circular, a road once dotted with truck stops and cafes frequented by Mods, Rockers, bikers, Jazzers and Skifflers and other 'outsider' groups of youth culture, he also explained that a grove denotes a collective term for a group of druids, which to me seemed to lend and deepen a historical, as well as cultural, significance to the Grove DiY project. As well as re-claiming the parking lot, the volunteers at The Grove have dug and started a community garden on the premises, growing vegetables and other plants for community use.

Crab Tacos

A glug of olive oil
A knob of butter
Half a bulb of fresh fennel (finely chopped)
3 or 4 sun dried tomatoes from a jar (finely chopped)
A pinch of dried chilli flakes
A 230g tin of cannellini beans
A glass of white wine
220g mixed, white and brown cooked crab meat
A pinch of salt and plenty of fresh ground black pepper
6 soft taco wraps
Grated cheddar cheese

Heat the oil and melt the butter in a frying pan over a moderate heat and add the chopped fennel. Cook for two or three minutes, until the fennel begins to soften. Throw in the chopped sun dried tomatoes and the chilli flakes. Add the beans and the wine and stir gently. Turn the heat down and simmer for a further four minutes allowing the sauce to thicken slightly. Turn off the heat and using a fork stir in the crab meat. Season to taste with salt and pepper. Spoon a little of the filling on to the tacos, scatter with grated cheddar and melt under a hot grill.

STALEFISH
NO CHIPS

With time out between conference presentations, We also managed a ride up to La Jolla with ex pro skater and pal of Brian Glenney's, Dan Rogers who took us via the Don Bravo Grill & Cantina, where I sampled a crab taco for the first time in my life, and bought a natty blue baseball cap. I have to admit that the crab taco was among the many highlights of the trip.

Fresh recipe ideas aside, the San Diego trip reaffirmed my interest in skateboarding academia, but more importantly, it furnished me with a bunch of new friends and a renewed enthusiasm for throwing myself into situations where I don't necessarily know people without worrying about whether things will work out. I guess that in some ways sums up skateboarding - just drop in and go with the flow.

Dr. M. L. King WAY 900 W →

SERVICE
TO OTHERS IS
THE RENT YOU
PAY FOR YOUR
ROOM HERE ON
EARTH

POLITICS IS
CORRUPT
ANYBODY KNOWS THAT
IT'S A BRAVE NEW WORLD
WE'RE LIVING IN
SO HOW DOES IT FEEL TO HAVE
A SOCIAL ENGINEERING WAR
BEING FOISTED ON YOU!?

DISSENT Is The
Highest Form
Of PATRIOTISM.

I THINK I SHALL NEVER SEE A POEM AS LOVELY AS A TREE Joyce Kilmer   DON'T LOOK BACK...
SOMETHING MIGHT BE
GAINING ON YOU Satchel Paige

LONDON CALLING

LONDON 17-20 AUG 2023

London calling, yes I was there too and you know what they said? Well some of it was true. In fact it was probably all true, it's just that as I didn't take up skateboarding until I was in my fifties, I couldn't really vouch for what happened on the emerging UK skateboarding scene in the 1970s.

There was never any doubt that when Steve Douglas, Bod Boyle, Don Brown and Dan Adams put out the call to the faraway towns, that all the boys and girls would come out of the cupboard. London Calling was an outstanding success, and the fact that DEVO were playing one of their last ever gigs at Hammersmith Apollo on the same weekend just seemed fitting. The event was conceived and put together as a tribute to the original pioneers of the UK skate scene which emerged in the mid/late1970s. Held in London over the weekend of 17-20 august, it kicked off with an exhibition of photographs and video footage, much of which had not been shown in public before. The walls of the Pure Evil Gallery on Leonard Street were adorned with posters, magazine covers, skateboards and other paraphernalia associated with the emergent phenomenon. To mark the event Vans had issued a special retro edition of the red and blue shoes which many of the riders in the photographs and videos could be seen wearing at the time. I picked up a copy of the accompanying zine, a fantastic compendium of much of the exhibition material packed with words from the original riders. With Alex Turnbull playing music by The Slits, Siouxsie & the Banshees, the B52s and of course, the Clash, the gallery was packed with skaters my own age and older, stepping back in time but revelling in reunions of the present day. I wasn't quite sure, but could have sworn that Alex managed to slip a little 23 Skidoo into the mix towards the end of the evening.

As a later skater I've met many new friends, and built enduring friendships cemented by a love for skateboarding. As a practical stranger in the room at the Pure Evil Gallery on the Thursday evening I was moved by the sheer amount of love in the room. Hugs and handshakes separated by decades and smiles that bridged the years like these people had last seen each other only yesterday. And as a skater, I felt part of it all, taken under the wings of veterans.

The following morning we all went to university. Under the guiding arm of Iain Borden, professor of architecture and urban culture at UCL, himself a skater and co-conspirator in the London Calling politburo, we were directed to a lecture hall in the cruciform building on Gower Street. Here in the reception area I detected an underlying yorkshire accent poking through a Californian twang. Curious, I introduced myself and met Andy Lomas, originally from Leeds and now living in Arizona, via California.

Keen to hear tales of my home town and some early Leeds skate history I asked him when he first started skating. After picking up his first board in 1976, he soon got a job at Truckstop in the Merrion Centre, where he began to meet other skateboarders from around the west Yorkshire area, leading to an emerging northern skateboarding scene that would lay challenge to its southern counterpart, LSD - London Skates Dominate and claim Leeds Skates Dominate!

Moving through to the lecture hall, I met Andy's friends and fellow northern skaters Stefan Harkon, and the Burdell siblings Sheenagh and Darren. Our conversation continued as the lecture hall filled up. With Freddie Laker offering one way flights to the US for less than a hundred pounds (roughly the equivalent of £700 today) aboard his 'Skytrain', Andy, like a number of other UK skaters managed to squirrel the money for a trip to California in 1978. Andy didn't come back. Darren told me he was less fortunate, after returning to England for a short family visit, his attempt to get back into the States was refused when immigration officers found a letter from his American girlfriend confirming that the (illegal) job had been kept open and everyone at work was looking forward to his return. He was put on the next flight home.

Having never actually heard of these skateboard pioneers and legends, owing to my delayed entry into the skateboarding world and consequently skating with people some twenty, even thirty years younger than myself, it's tales like these that re-affirm my enthusiasm for skateboarding. That pioneering, 'hell let's just go for it attitude' can be found at the heart of skateboard culture.

The lecture hall filled to capacity and over the next three hours two panels of pioneers including Jeremy Henderson, John Sablosky, Ben Liddell, Kadir Guirey, Marc Sinclair, Alex Turnbull, Simon Napper, Sheenagh Burdell, James Cassimus and Tony Alva, all took their place on the forum at the front of the hall. The session was joined via Zoom by Mark Baker and Steve Olson from Mark's home in Bali.

What was clear from the conversations was that the UK skaters were obviously inspired by their American counterparts, but lacking the parks and facilities across the Atlantic they learned to skate in their own environment, the undercroft at Southbank on the Thames, on derelict land at Meanwhile Gardens and on emerging new skateparks, Skate City and Harrow. "Our environment shaped our style," Andy Lomas whispered in my ear as I sat next to him. Equally the Americans, especially those that visited back in the day, were stoked on the UK scene. Tony Alva claimed that in 1978 skating the UK spots and bowls around the country, all a far cry from the quality of American facilities that he was used to, gave him the foundation to dominate in France. After skating England, he said, all the other stuff he encountered in Europe seemed easier. He also said that the food was so terrible that even that toughened him up.

Glancing around the filled room I took joy, marvelling at peoples' faces, filled with smiles and respect for the panel of original skaters sat at the front of this lecture hall. To be honest, I'd been a little trepidatious about coming to this gig. None of my much younger contemporaries on the Leeds scene had shown any interest, and why should they? Separated by so many decades. But for me, a lot closer in age to those radicals, it was different and I can explain it like this; if my discovery of skateboarding could be compared with the equivalent of discovering the Clash for the first time, then my time at London Calling was akin to discovering the Beatles, the Stones and the Small Faces, those pioneers that in turn inspired Jones and Strummer et al.

Most of the old crew met at Southbank for a session the following day, then again at the DEVO concert in the evening. I managed to say a final cheerio to Andy Lomas and threw a nod in Tony Alva's direction as we were ushered through the VIP doors into the venue and up to the green room, "you coming in?" asked Andy, no I said, "I'm Not Down" and went off to enjoy the gig from the cheap seats. London Calling hit the top of the dial, and after all this, there were plenty of smiles, especially at the meet-up on Sunday down at Crystal Palace, but by then I was heading to Stockwell in my Pink Cadillac.

Stockwell Park happens to be one of my favourite places to skate in London. Originally built in 1978, it has recently been refurbished by Betongpark ltd who also had a big hand in improving Hackney Bumps. The recent re-surfacing covered the old and extremely gnarly grey concrete and saw it turn (back) to red. Opting to ride Stockwell rather than join all the veteran skaters up a South Bank by the river (largely because I find South Bank too hard to skate and the fact that everyone would be out of my league) meant that I got to hook up with a bunch of pals I'd not seen for a good while, including Nick, who was a fellow volunteer with me out in Palestine, as well as Paul, who I'd first met back in San Diego and Simon from the Shoreham crew I met on the pool tour.

Ingredients:

A dash of vegetable oil
3 cloves of garlic (finely chopped)
A similar amount of fresh root ginger (peeled and finely chopped)
6 chestnut mushrooms (finely sliced)
1 red pepper (de-deed and finely sliced)
1 tsp dark soy sauce
2 tsp light soy sauce
3 tbsp of black bean sauce
225g smoked tofu (sliced and cut into thin shreds)

Heat the oil in a frying pan and throw in the chopped garlic and ginger. Give it a quick stir to spread those flavours around the oil in the pan, then throw in the chopped mushrooms and peppers. As soon as the mushrooms begin to soak up the oil, add the two types of soy sauce and the black bean sauce too. Finally throw in the tofu and give it a good stir to coat everything in the sauce. Stir fry for just a couple of minutes and serve on a bed of noodles.

For the noodles

A dash of sesame oil
Half of the chopped garlic
Half of the chopped ginger
300g fresh egg noodles
1 tsp dark soy sauce
2 tsp light soy sauce

Heat the oil in a wok, or large frying pan. Throw in the garlic and ginger and as soon as the wonderful aromas hit the nose, chuck in the noodles and the soy sauce and give it all a good stir. The noodles are already cooked, so you're just heating them up really, but the flavours of the ginger, soy and garlic will really lift them.

STUFFED RED PEPPERS

Ingredients:

4 Red Peppers
A knob of butter
Olive oil
1 onion (finely chopped)
2 cloves garlic (peeled and chopped)
200g mushrooms (chopped)
Salt & Black pepper
1tsp smoked paprika
225g basmati rice
400ml vegetable stock
A handful of fresh flat leaf parsley (chopped)
A tin of chopped tomatoes

Drizzle a little olive oil in a frying pan and add the knob of butter and simmer the chopped onion until it begins to caramelise. Next add the chopped garlic and the mushrooms. Add the paprika and plenty of ground black pepper. Give it a stir before adding the rice then mix through coating all of the rice. Pour in the vegetable stock and turn to a low heat to simmer gently, stirring gently from time to time.

While the rice is cooking, cut the tops from the peppers and scoop out the seeds. Pre-heat the oven to 180°C. Once the rice is cooked, remove from the heat and fill the peppers with the cooked rice, placing the 'lid' of the pepper on top. Pour the tin of tomatoes into an oven proof dish, season with salt & pepper and arrange the stuffed peppers in the dish. Place in the oven and bake for 40 minutes.

A CONCLUSION

SKATEBOARDADA

Die Kunst ist tot, es lebe die neue Maschinenkunst

This on-going journey into skateboarding has taken me far and wide, covering many miles countries and continents. Skateboarding continues to fascinate, enthuse and enthral me and I am nothing short of flabbergasted at the number of new friends, acquaintances and skills I've learned since I first stepped on a board six years ago. The experience has fuelled my creativity, in a way becoming a four-wheeled muse, leading to my setting-up of Red Fez Books - skater owned, skater focussed independent publishing, which now has five authors and seven titles on the list and selling in skate shops up and down the country. I've written for several skate zines, both online and in print. I've been writing and compiling this book for four years now, having set it aside to focus on publishing other peoples' material, but searching for a way to conclude I have become increasingly obsessed with what skateboarding actually is. I'm not sure that I am anywhere near being able to define it, but it strikes me that it shares a degree of similarity with an art movement that emerged in the early part of the twentieth century.

DaDa/ˈdaːdaː/ n. An early 20th.c international movement in art, literature, music and film, repudiating and mocking artistic and social conventions. (OED)

What is skateboarding? A subculture, sport, a way of life, art, a political act. These are all terms that have been used to describe skateboarding over the years, both by those who do it and those who don't. It's an on-going debate to be heard on the fringes of skateparks and spots the world over, and one that is unlikely ever to be settled. It mimics a debate that emerged as a result of the actions of a group of artists in the early part of the twentieth century, one which also to this day has arguably not been satisfactorily resolved. In 1913 a French artist, Marcel Duchamp, took what once was a piece of furniture and repurposed it by attaching a bicycle wheel set in an upturned pair of front forks on top of it. The wheel was able to spin freely, which amused Duchamp. In a similar way, skateboarders have learned to 'repurpose' furniture by skating benches, and handrails in the street for their own amusement. There is something defiant but also humorous in taking an everyday object and redefining its purpose.

Origin stories are important. Often emerging a number of years following the phenomenon that they describe, they shape the way that we come to look at things and lend credence to their history. Just three years after fixing a wheel to his stool, Duchamp found himself among a group of artists, writers, performers and poets in Europe who were defying artistic convention to such an extent that some among them would claim that art is dead, DaDa Lives! Origin stories also carry a degree of ambiguity which feeds their importance, as it allows for a range of interpretations and therefore 'meanings' or significance to those who practice or admire the subject of the story itself. The origins of DaDa for example, are often explained as a reaction to the atrocity of the First World War, or as emanating from a revulsion to emerging twentieth century society and artistic convention. Even the origin of the name DaDa itself lacks consensus, one story being that the name was plucked at random from a dictionary by German Artist and Philosopher, Richard Huelsenbeck, another suggests that Tristan Tzara, or perhaps Hugo Ball coined the term. The uncertainty feeds into, and becomes part of the story.

The origin story of modern skateboarding revolves around the legend of a skate team comprising a group of surfers who sought an alternative pastime when the surf was flat. Written by Stacey Peralta and Craig Stecyk and directed by Peralta, the 2001 film Dog Town and Z-Boys has shaped the origin story and cemented the idea that skateboarders are unconventional, outsiders with little respect for the rules of the game. As described in the film, the style that the Zephyr Skate team brought to early skateboard competition mocked artistic and social convention. The film goes on to describe how the skaters began draining and skating swimming pools for entertainment, challenging authority and private land owners through re-purposing what some might see as a symbol of wealth, the privately owned back yard swimming pool.

A challenge to decadence. Just as DaDa had shocked audiences with its unconventional nature half a century previously, skateboarders were now redefining the parameters of skateboarding itself. However, again in common with DaDa, this particular zeitgeist was short-lived. As quarrels and disagreements among the practitioners of DaDa lead to its demise, similarly the Zephyr team drifted from Dogtown into Dog Day Afternoon as loyalties slipped, the plan fell apart and hard cash tempted team members abroad to other teams and brands.

Yet despite its temporary nature, DaDa had a profound and lasting influence in both the art world and, consequently, in that of skateboarding. The fact that DaDa was not confined to any one particular artistic discipline goes some way to explaining how and why its influence on skateboarding has been so easily absorbed. DaDa was expressed through art, literature, music, poetry, film and performance, all of which are also now embedded within modern skateboard culture. Echos of Hannah Hoch's photomontage and Duchamp's 'Ready Mades', the idea of repurposing an object to suit one's needs, emerged later, visible in the Situationist notion of Détournement in the 1960s. The 'hijacking' of images or objects and repurposing them, adapting them to one's own, often provocative, ends is one that sits well within skateboarding culture. As street furniture is repurposed by skaters themselves, to create skate spots (often provoking anger among the public, property owners and hired 'insecurity' personnel), so too are images 'hijacked' by artists producing skateboard graphics. Their repurposing of religious, political and corporate iconography to provocative and satirical effect can be seen as reflective of DaDa's desire to challenge the world around it. Skaterdemic (skater/academic) Dr Paul O'Connor notes in his book, Skateboarding and Religion (Palgrave McMillan: 2020) how skateboard graphics have a significant history of being subversive and satirical;

"In using satire, skateboard graphics reinforce skateboarders as an alternative heterodox culture, interested not simply in rejecting convention, but more importantly in questioning the norms of society and striving to see the world differently." (O'Connor: 2020)

Die Kunst ist tot, es lebe die neue Maschinenkunst

In 1991, satirical turned satanical with Marc Mckee's graphic for 101 Skateboards, which ended up as the Natas Kaupas Devil Worship deck. Complete with pentagram, headless baby, pope on a rope and Old Nick himself sitting cross (goat) legged centre stage, the graphic raised a few eyebrows to say the least, most certainly questioning the norms of not just skateboard graphics at the time, but society as a whole. At the time of its release, 101 took out an advert in Thrasher magazine with Kaupas' hand written note; 'But seriously folks, these are jokes. These are all jokes'.

More recently, Jon Horner's 'Nye Bevan, Patron Saint of UK Skateboarding' graphic for Lovenskate (2019) provides a wonderful example of satire within a political context as the National Health Service in Britain is being systematically destroyed by the Tory government, the canonisation of its founding father serves to raise a laugh, as well as the profile of the state of the NHS itself, which of course British skateboarders rely on from time to time to patch them up after injury.

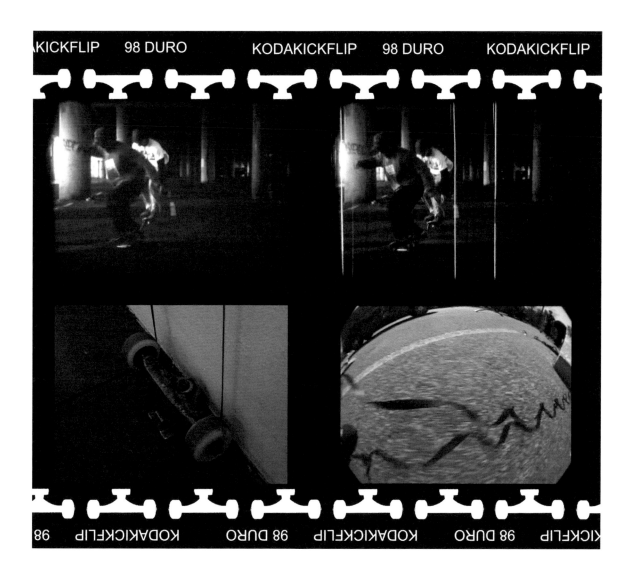

When motion film was developed as a new medium early in the twentieth century, artists were quick to adopt it. DaDaist Hans Richter's film Rhythmus 21 was shown in Paris in 1921. Lasting approximately three minutes, it shows a set of rectangular shapes in stop frame motion moving to and from the foreground, becoming larger and smaller as the shapes appear to move closer and further away from the camera. It depicts movement in a seemingly abstract manner that leaves the viewer with a sense of travel. Similarly, Duchamp's Anémic Cinéma (1926) shows a number of circular shapes rotating, again invoking a sense of travel. Both showcase a new technique, or trick if you like. Skate videos, which first began to appear in the early 1980s, showcase tricks performed by riders and a continual sense of movement or travel.

In the case of The Search for Animal Chin (Directed by Stacey Peralta in 1987) the film also carries with it a playful sense of the absurd within the story line via search for the mythical character 'Won Ton "Animal" Chin'. By the 1990s the notion of absurdity and with it an underlying sense of satirical humour in skate films was becoming more common. Spike Jones' 'Mouse' (1997) opens with a giant mouse riding a skateboard through the streets much to the bemusement and occasional horror of the general public. The assisted rail ride and leap to the pavement strikes terror and tears into the eyes of two young children apparently out shopping with their mother.

The film is packed with a combination of humorous skits and sick tricks performed by the riders for Girl Skateboards and goes some way toward mocking the artistic convention of skate film making as a whole.

Much more recently, in a film which debuted at The Stoke Sessions Conference held at San Diego State University (2023) that notion of travel and tricks is captured and portrayed in a visual manner not dissimilar to the early DaDa films of Richter et al. Presented in a quad frame format on the screen, Skate Scratch (Cunningham and Dixon, 2023) destroys the traditional format of a skate film, while at the same time expanding the audiovisual experience for the viewer, inviting them to see and hear this world from a different perspective. One frame of the film shows a skater trailing the developed cine-film around a skatepark, scratching and subjecting it to abuse that could quite possibly render it useless. The scratched and abused film, as well as the same film, prior to being deliberately damaged, run in the top half of the screen depicting a skater performing a series of tricks. The bottom half of the screen depicts footage of the abuse itself, as well as footage of the sound engineer (Dixon) running the audio recording via an extended tape loop through a number of effect pedals and other electronic jiggery pokery. The motive behind the making of this extraordinary film was not entirely clear, other than the fact that doing so was possible. I would describe it as skateboarDaDa. Cunningham, Wyatt & Dixon, Ben. (2023). Skate Scratch. YouTube.

Retrieved May 30, 2023, from https://www.youtube.com/watch?v=SP8JSG-8Bmg

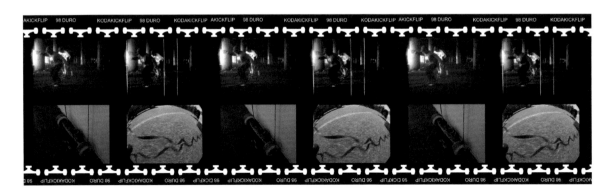

Modern skateboard culture, like DaDa over half a century before it, is manifest through a range of media driven by a strong Do it Yourself ethic. Zines present a low-cost means of participating in, and contributing to this culture. The DiY approach adopted by the DaDaists, from the opening of the Cabaret Voltaire in Zurich in 1916 and the production of individual manifestos and booklets, is also mirrored in the practice of skateboarders today. DiY skateparks built by and for skaters themselves present an arena in which they are able to perform, while the manufacture and distribution of zines presents a means of reaching a broader audience. The cut and paste approach to skate zine production, evident in early DaDa publications, was prevalent during the 1980s in the pre-digital age. The advent of desktop publishing programmes and cheap online digital printing has furthered and strengthened the position of zines as a cornerstone of skate culture. Titles like Two Set, Confusion, Filthy Ditch Crew, Tomb Crawler, Across tides, Vague and myriad others are meticulously put together by individuals with contributions from skaters offering essays and articles which go beyond the standard interview format of mainstream skate journalism.

The commonality between Skateboarding and DaDa, from the ambiguity of definition, to the heterodox nature of the phenomenon itself, leads me to conclude that the two are intrinsically linked. Of course, those who are unaware of the movement started by a group of artists shortly after the turn of the twentieth century may not be aware of any such link. I think it was Hugo Ball who said, 'Before there was DaDa, DaDa was there'. In turn I say that before there was skateboarding, skateboarding was there. To put it another way, Skateboarding is dead - long live SkateboarDaDa

BIBLIOGRAPHY

Books:

Abulhawa, D: Skateboarding and Femininity, Routledge, Oxford: 2020
Beachy, K, *The Most Fun Thing*, Grand Central Publishing, New York: 2021
Borden, I: *Skateboarding and the City*, Bloomsbury, London: 2019
Borden, I: *Skateboarding, space and the Cit, y*Berg, Oxford: 2001
Cliver, S: *Disposable - a history of skateboard art*, Gingko Press, Berkley: 2004
Friedel, S: *The Art of Living Sideways: Skateboarding, peace and elicitive conflict transformation*, Springer, New York: 2015
Gilligan, R. *DIY/Underground Skateparks*, (Prestel, London: DATE?)
Lombard, K.J (ed): *Skateboarding, subcultures, sites and shifts*, Routledge, London and New York: 2016
Mullen, R" *The Mutt*, Dey St, USA: 2004
O'Connor, P, Skateboarding and Religion, Palgrave Macmillan, Cham: 2020
O'Connor, P, *'Skateboard Philanthropy: Inclusion and prefigurative politics'* in K-J Lombard, (ed.), Skate boarding: Subcultures, Sites and Shifts, Routledge, London and New York, 30-43.
Richter, H, *Dada - art and anti-art*, Thames & Hudson, London:1970
Roden, C, *A New Book of Middle Eastern Food*, Penguin, London: 1970
Sutton, J: *CookPal*, Red Fez Books, Otley: 2018
Rooum, D. *What is Anarchism - an introduction,* (Freedom Press, London: 1992)
Spowart & Burrows *Negotiating Moral Terrain: Snowboarding Mothers,* in Women in Action Sport Cultures: Holly Thorpe, Rebecca Olive (eds.) Palgrave Macmillan: 2016

Zines:

Döner, (2019). Bellamy, J.
Roll with the punches (2017). Bird, T.
Out of the Blues, (March 2019) issue No.1. Jacob, L.
Skateism, various issues
Vague, various issues
Skate Pal Magazine, issue 1 (2017)
Across Tides, issue 1 (2020)
Grey, Vol 5, issue 6

Journals:

Holly Thorpe and Robert Rinehart, (2013), *'Action Sports NGOs in a Neo-liberal Context: The cases of Skateistan and Surf Aid International'*, **Journal of Sport and Social Issues, 37(2), 115-141.**

Bridgman, S, Collins, J. & Collins, D. F. (1992). *Human body motion in an ollie.* **The Physics Teacher, 30(8), 498-499.**

Ocean Howell *The "Creative Class" and the Gentrifying City: Skateboarding in Philadelphia's Love Park*: **Journal of Architectural Education (1984-), Vol. 59, No. 2 (Nov., 2005), pp. 32-42**

Websites:

https://www.greyskatemag.com/post/the-freedom-skatepark-interview-building-kingstons-first-skatepark-in-the-midst-of-the-covid-19-pandemic/skatejawn.com

Cunningham, W & Dixon, B; https://www.youtube.com/watch?v=SP8JSG-8Bmg

O'Connor, P; Beyond the youth culture : understanding middle-aged skateboarders through temporal capital (2017): https://commons.ln.edu.hk/cgi/viewcontent.cgi?referer=http://scholar.google.co.uk/&httpsredir=1&article=6232&context=sw_master

Mullen, Rodney, TED Talk October 2013 (https://www.youtube.com/watch?v=DBbmNAZWq-E)

Sayers, E, *Motion as Material* (film): https://tenderfoot.co.uk/motion-as-material/

BUTTER BEANS ON TOAST
smörgåsBOARD

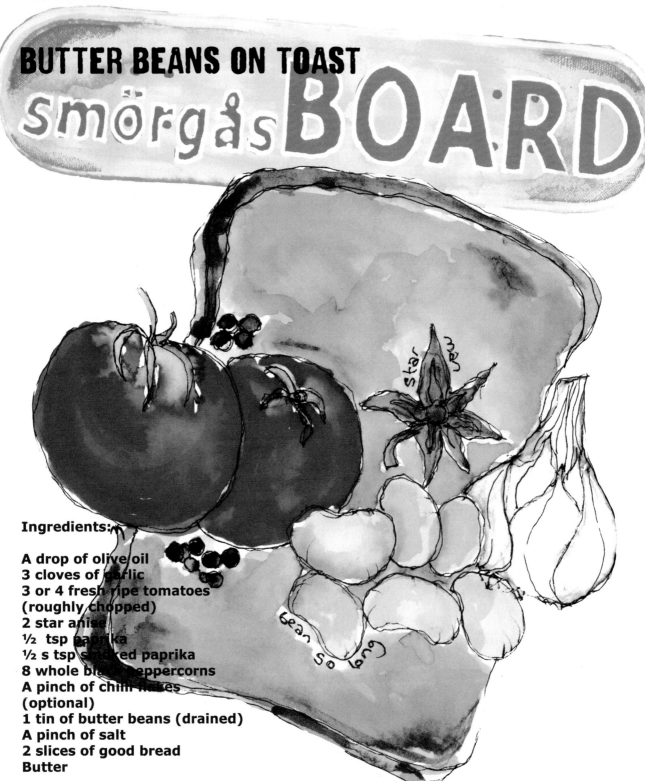

Ingredients:

A drop of olive oil
3 cloves of garlic
3 or 4 fresh ripe tomatoes
(roughly chopped)
2 star anise
½ tsp paprika
½ s tsp smoked paprika
8 whole black peppercorns
A pinch of chilli flakes
(optional)
1 tin of butter beans (drained)
A pinch of salt
2 slices of good bread
Butter

Peel and fine chop the garlic and fry in a little olive oil until it begins to colour. Add the
chopped fresh tomatoes, together with the star anise, paprika and peppercorns (and
the chilli flakes if you're up for it). Lower the heat and simmer until the tomatoes
begin to break down. Add the drained butter beans and the salt and simmer gently for
another five minutes. Toast your bread and spread with good butter. Remove the star
anise and serve the beans on hot buttered toast.